SCRATCH™ PROGRAMMING FOR TEENS

JERRY LEE FORD, JR.

Course Technology PTR

A part of Cengage Learning

COURSE TECHNOLOGY
CENGAGE Learning™

Australia • Brazil • Japan • Korea • Mexico • Singapore • Spain • United Kingdom • United States

COURSE TECHNOLOGY
CENGAGE Learning™

Scratch™ Programming for Teens
Jerry Lee Ford, Jr.

Publisher and General Manager, Course Technology PTR: Stacy L. Hiquet

Associate Director of Marketing: Sarah Panella

Manager of Editorial Services: Heather Talbot

Marketing Manager: Mark Hughes

Acquisitions Editor: Mitzi Koontz

Project Editor: Jenny Davidson

Technical Reviewer: Parker Hiquet

Teen Reviewer: Hannah Wittig

PTR Editorial Services Coordinator: Erin Johnson

Interior Layout Tech: ICC Macmillan Inc.

Cover Designer: Mike Tanamachi

CD-ROM Producer: Brandon Penticuff

Indexer: Sharon Shock

Proofreader: Gene Redding

© 2009 Course Technology, a part of Cengage Learning.

ALL RIGHTS RESERVED. No part of this work covered by the copyright herein may be reproduced, transmitted, stored, or used in any form or by any means graphic, electronic, or mechanical, including but not limited to photocopying, recording, scanning, digitizing, taping, Web distribution, information networks, or information storage and retrieval systems, except as permitted under Section 107 or 108 of the 1976 United States Copyright Act, without the prior written permission of the publisher.

For product information and technology assistance, contact us at **Cengage Learning Customer & Sales Support, 1-800-354-9706**

For permission to use material from this text or product, submit all requests online at **cengage.com/permissions**
Further permissions questions can be e-mailed to
permissionrequest@cengage.com

Scratch is a project of the Lifelong Kindergarten group at the MIT Media Lab. Scratch, the Scratch logo, and the Scratch cat are trademarks of the Massachusetts Institute of Technology.
All other trademarks are the property of their respective owners.

All images © Cengage Learning unless otherwise noted.

Library of Congress Control Number: 2008902386

ISBN-13: 978-1-59863-536-2

ISBN-10: 1-59863-536-0

Course Technology
25 Thomson Place
Boston, MA 02210
USA

Cengage Learning is a leading provider of customized learning solutions with office locations around the globe, including Singapore, the United Kingdom, Australia, Mexico, Brazil, and Japan. Locate your local office at: **international.cengage.com/region**

Cengage Learning products are represented in Canada by Nelson Education, Ltd.

For your lifelong learning solutions, visit **courseptr.com**

Visit our corporate website at **cengage.com**

Printed by Webcom, Toronto, Ontario, Canada. 2nd Ptr. 10/2009

Printed in the United States of America
4 5 6 7 12 11

To my mother and father for always being there, and to my wonderful children, Alexander, William, and Molly, and my beautiful wife, Mary.

Acknowledgments

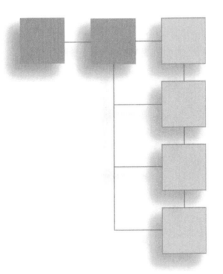

There are a number of individuals to whom I owe many thanks for their help and assistance in the development of this book. For starters I need to thank Mitzi Koontz who served as the book's acquisitions editor. Special thanks also go out to Jenny Davidson for serving as the book's project editor. I also want to thank Parker Hiquet and Hannah Wittig for all the valuable input and advice. In addition, I would like to thank everyone else at Cengage Learning for all their hard work.

Special thanks to the Scratch development team at the MIT Media Lab for providing such an excellent programming langauge and website.

ABOUT THE AUTHOR

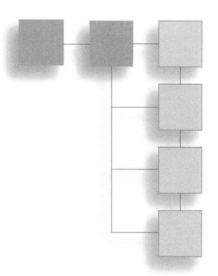

Jerry Lee Ford, Jr. is an author, educator, and an IT professional with over 18 years' experience in information technology, including roles as an automation analyst, technical manager, technical support analyst, automation engineer, and security analyst. He is the author of 24 other books and co-author of two additional books. His published works include *AppleScript Studio Programming for the Absolute Beginner, Microsoft Windows PowerShell Programming for the Absolute Beginner, Microsoft Visual Basic 2005 Express Edition Programming for the Absolute Beginner, Microsoft VBScript Professional Projects, Microsoft Windows Shell Scripting and WSH Administrator's Guide, Microsoft Windows Shell Script Programming for the Absolute Beginner, Learn JavaScript in a Weekend, Second Edition,* and *Microsoft Windows XP Professional Administrator's Guide.* Jerry has a master's degree in business administration from Virginia Commonwealth University in Richmond, Virginia, and he has over five years' experience as an adjunct instructor teaching networking courses in information technology.

Contents

INTRODUCTION

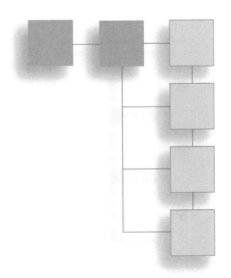

Welcome to *Scratch Programming for Teens!* Scratch is a programming language developed by the MIT Media Lab for the purpose of teaching programming to teens and other first-time programmers. Scratch is a new programming language, initially released in May 2007. Scratch supports the development of computer games, interactive stories, graphic artwork and computer animation, and all sorts of other multimedia projects.

Scratch allows new programmers to create programs by snapping together blocks. Scratch consists of a programming language made up of different blocks and an easy to learn graphical development environment that includes a paint application for creating graphics and built-in sound editing capabilities. Scratch also comes with huge collections of sample applications as well as graphics and sound files, all of which you can use to create your own Scratch projects.

As demonstrated in Figure A.1, Scratch programs are made up of graphical blocks, which are snapped together. Scratch blocks resemble puzzle pieces in the way that they snap together. Scratch blocks can only be snapped together in ways that make sense, preventing new programmers from using them in invalid combinations. In this way, Scratch enforces proper programming syntax and ensures that new programmers learn the proper way to assemble and formulate programming logic.

Scratch's development was inspired by the method that hip-hop DJs use to mix and scratch records to create new and unique music. In Scratch, new programmers

Figure A.1
Script blocks are used as the basis for writing scripts that help bring applications to life.

are able to create new application projects that incorporate pre-built code blocks, graphics, and sound files in all kinds of new combinations. Scratch lets programmers modify applications on the fly, allowing changes to be made even while Scratch applications are running. The result is an interactive, real-time programming environment that encourages experimentation and learning.

This book's primary goal is to teach you everything you need to know to learn the basics of computer programming with Scratch. To help accomplish this goal, this book will emphasize learning by doing through the development of a series of fun and interesting exercises.

Why Scratch?

Scratch provides everything needed to begin developing computer games, multimedia presentations, interactive stories, graphic artwork, and computer animation. Scratch can be used to play digital music and sound effects. Scratch's building block approach to programming sets it apart from other programming languages. This makes Scratch easier to learn. And yet Scratch provides plenty of programming power, allowing you to build very powerful application projects.

If you aspire to one day become a professional programmer, you will find that Scratch provides everything needed to build a foundation from which you can make the transition. Scratch also packs all of the programming power and punch needed to satisfy the programming needs of most computer enthusiasts and hobbyists.

Who Should Read This Book?

Scratch Programming for Teens is designed to provide all of the instruction that a first-time programmer requires to quickly get up and running. Previous programming experience will certainly be helpful, but it is by no means a requirement of this book. This book makes no assumptions about your computer background other than that you are comfortable working with one of the operations systems supported by Scratch.

This book provides everything you need to get started with Scratch. Before you know it, you will be creating all kinds of projects, incorporating graphics, sound, and animation. As you learn how to program with Scratch, you will learn programming principles and techniques that you can later apply to other programming languages. As such, you will be able to apply what you learn about programming with Scratch to other programming languages like Microsoft Visual Basic and AppleScript.

What You Need to Begin

Obviously, the first thing you need is a copy of Scratch. Scratch is available for free download at the Scratch website located at http://scratch.mit.edu/download. You can also download a copy from the CD included in the back of the book. You also need good instruction, which you will find in this book. In addition to Scratch and this book, you need a computer running a supported operating system, which also meets Scratch's minimum system requirements.

Supported Operating Systems

Scratch can be run on computers using either Microsoft or Macintosh operating systems. Specifically, Scratch can be installed on a computer running any of the following operating systems.

- Microsoft Windows 98/ME

- Microsoft Windows NT/2000

- Microsoft Windows XP/Vista

- Mac OS X Version 10.3 or higher

All of the figures and examples in this book will be shown using Scratch 1.2.1 running on computers using either Microsoft Vista or Mac OS X 10.5. If you are going to be working with Scratch on a different version of Windows or Mac OS X, you may notice small differences in the way things look. However, all major Scratch features and functionality should work the same and you should not have any problems following along with the instruction provided in this book.

Note

There is no official Linux version of Scratch currently available. However, members of the Scratch community have created different Scratch implementations for Linux. An example of one such implementation is available at http://tcpdpodcast.org/scratch.html.

Minimum System Requirements

Scratch does not impose any additional hardware requirements over and above those required by the operating system. However, as Table A.1 shows, Scratch does impose screen resolution and disk space requirements, which must be met for Scratch to run.

To work with Scratch, you must be able to display its graphical interface, also referred to as its *integrated development environment* or *IDE*. This interface requires that the computer's screen resolution be set to 1024 × 768 or higher. Anything less and part of the interface will disappear off the screen. Scratch comes packed with all kinds of graphics and audio files that you can use when creating new Scratch projects. As a result, your computer must have at least an extra 120 MB of hard disk space in order to install Scratch.

Note

One of the really neat things about Scratch is the ability to share Scratch application projects with others on the Internet at the Scratch website (Scratch.mit.edu). To participate in this experience, your computer needs to have Java installed. Mac OS X comes with Java pre-installed. However, by default, Microsoft Windows does not. So, if you are a Windows user and you have not yet installed Java on your computer, you can do so by visiting http://java.com/en/download.index.jsp.

Table A.1 Scratch Minimum System Requirements

Requirement	Recommended
Screen Resolution	1024 × 768 (16-bit color)
Hard Disk	120 MB

Of course, Scratch's minimum hardware requirements are just that, minimum requirements. If your computer's memory and processor exceed the minimum requirements of the operating system, things will run a lot faster and you will be a lot happier. In addition, you will need extra hard drive space beyond the 120 MB minimum required to install Scratch to have a place to store your creations. Scratch lets you create projects that incorporate the use of sound, both as input and output. To take advantage of this feature, your computer will need both speakers and a microphone.

How This Book Is Organized

Scratch Programming for Teens is organized into four parts. This book was written with the expectation that you will read it sequentially, from cover to cover. However, if you have some previous programming experience, you may instead want to jump around a bit, focusing on topics that interest you the most.

Part I of this book is made up of four chapters that provide an introduction to Scratch and its development environment. You will also learn about the different components that make up Scratch projects and then learn how to create and execute Scratch projects.

Part II consists of eight chapters, each of which is designed to provide instruction on how to work with different types of Scratch blocks. You will learn how to use blocks that move things around, store and retrieve data, as well as perform math and conditional and repetitive logic. You will also learn how to integrate sound and draw lines and shapes.

Part III of this book is made up of three chapters, each of which focuses on a different advanced topic. These topics include learning how to share your Scratch projects with others on the Internet, how to create Scratch projects that use the Scratch Board, and how to find and fix program errors that prevent your Scratch projects from working like you want them to.

Part IV is made up of two appendices and a glossary. The first appendix reviews the list of sample Scratch projects that you will learn how to develop as you make your way through this book. The second appendix provides a list of websites and reading materials that you will want to explore to continue learning more about Scratch and to further your programming knowledge.

Conventions Used in This Book

One of the primary objectives of this book is for it to be easy to read and understand. To help support this objective, a number of simple conventions have been used throughout the book to highlight critical information and help emphasize specific points. These conventions are briefly described below.

- *Italics.* Key terms that you will want to understand and remember are highlighted using italics the first time that they are instructed. So remember, anytime you see a term in italics, take an extra moment to think about it and understand its meaning or purpose.

Note

Notes are used to provide additional information about a topic, feature, or idea to better help you understand its impact or implications.

Tip

Tips are used to point out programming shortcuts that will help make you a better and more efficient programmer.

Caution

Cautions are used to identify areas where you are likely to run into problems and then provide advice on how to deal with the problem or prevent problems from occurring, making you a better, more efficient, and much happier programmer.

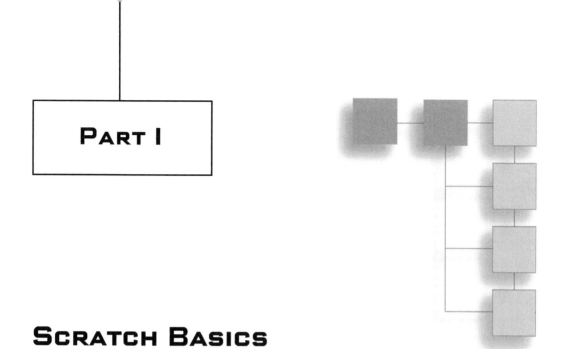

PART I

SCRATCH BASICS

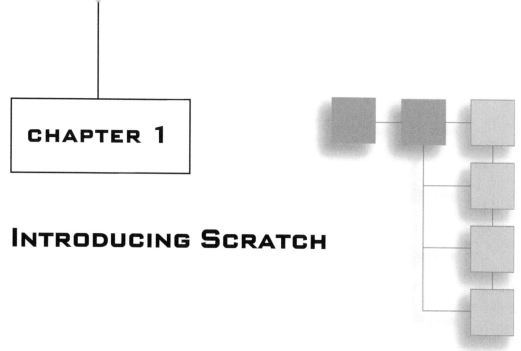

CHAPTER 1

INTRODUCING SCRATCH

Scratch is a programming language developed to help young people between the ages of 8 and 16 learn 21st century skills by developing computer programs. The development of Scratch was inspired by the scratching process that DJs use to create new sounds and music by rubbing old-style vinyl records back and forth on record turntables, creating a new and distinctively different sound out of something that already exists. In similar fashion, Scratch application projects mix together graphics and sounds in order to use them in new and different ways. To help get you started with Scratch programming, this chapter provides an overview of the language and reviews the steps that you need to follow to get up and running quickly.

The major topics covered in this chapter include:

- A review of Scratch's capabilities and uses

- Instruction on how to install Scratch on both Microsoft Windows and Mac OS X

- A discussion of the benefits of joining Scratch's global community

- A demonstration of how to create and execute your first Scratch application project

Getting to Know Scratch

With traditional computer and Internet applications, users are limited to working with applications in the way the programmers who developed the applications designed. Scratch turns things around by letting users become programmers. Scratch is designed to meet the needs of young people between 8 and 16, helping to introduce them to computer technology and to improve their learning skills while at the same time facilitating creativity and personal expression.

Many people regard computer programming as a mysterious and complex process that requires advanced technical training and education. This is a misperception. Programming languages like BASIC have been around for decades and were developed expressly for the purpose of teaching first-time programmers how to program. In recent years, a new crop of programming languages has appeared, specifically geared towards helping children and students learn to program. One of the very best and newest of these languages is Scratch.

Scratch is a visual programming language that is made up of a graphic interface that supports application development in which new projects are created by mixing together images, sound, and video under the control of scripts, which specify the application's programming logic. Scripts are created by snapping blocks together, much in the same way that Lego blocks are snapped together to create all sorts of unique creations. Each block represents a different command or action that tells the application how to execute. Scratch also provides programmers with access to all kinds of media, including graphics and sounds as well as tools that can be used to create new graphics and sound files.

Note

Scratch is also being installed on all XO laptops, as part of the One Laptop Per Child Project, which is a program designed to produce and distribute inexpensive laptop computers to children in developing countries around the world to help their education and unlock their potential.

Scratch is an interpreted programming language. This means that application projects are not precompiled (turned into executable code that can be run as a stand-alone application) before their execution. Instead, the code blocks that make up Scratch application projects are interpreted and processed each time the application project is executed. Scratch is also a dynamic programming language.

It allows changes to be made to application projects even while the projects are executing. As such, Scratch lets programmers experiment by making application changes on the fly in order to see what type of effect the changes may have on the application's execution.

Imagine—Program—Share!

Scratch's slogan is *Imagine—Program—Share!* It is designed to encourage teens' creativity by providing them with an easy to learn yet powerful programming environment in which they can unleash the power of their imagination. Scratch encourages and facilitates the development of application projects using a mixture of media, graphics, sound, and video in order to create something new.

Scratch provides new programmers with everything needed to create and execute new application projects. Its programming language is designed to make it as easy as possible for new programmers to jump in and get their feet wet and to receive immediate feedback on their progress. Scratch promotes an understanding of programming concepts, including conditional and iterative logic, event programming, the use of variables, mathematics, and the use of graphics, and sound effects. By learning to program with Scratch, new programmers develop an understanding and appreciation of the design process, from idea generation to program development, then testing and debugging and the incorporation of user feedback.

People, especially kids, love to share, as demonstrated through the amazing success of websites like YouTube, which allows people to share home video. Sharing is a fundamental part of the Scratch programming experience. Scratch application projects can not only be run on the programmer's desktop but can also be uploaded to the Scratch website, where they can be viewed, executed online, and commented on by other Scratch programmers from around the world. By posting their Scratch application projects on the Scratch website, kids share their experiences and learn from one another and gain gratification and confidence from the experience.

Hint

To share an application project, Scratch programmers must provide the source code that makes the application work. There is no way to keep the source code hidden.

Scratch Uncovered

For your convenience, a free trial copy of Scratch (version 1.2.1) is available on this book's companion CD-ROM. In addition, Scratch can be downloaded from the Scratch website located at http://scratch.mit.edu/download. Unlike many programming languages such as Microsoft Visual Basic or C++, Scratch is an open source project. What this means is that all of the source code that makes up the Scratch programming language is freely available. In fact, if you want, you can download a copy of the source code for Scratch at http://scratch.mit.edu/pages/source.

Note

Scratch was developed using another programming language known as Squeak. *Squeak* is a cross-platform programming language, meaning that it can be used to develop applications on many different computer operating systems. By selecting Squeak as the programming language used to create Scratch, Scratch's development team ensured that they would be able to create and execute Scratch on different operating systems, including Microsoft Windows and Mac OS X. If you are curious, you can learn more about Squeak by visiting http://www.squeak.org.

Examples of other open source programming languages include Ruby and Perl. However, unlike these programming languages developed by a community of programmers working together collectively, Scratch was developed as a closed development project. This means that all Scratch development is performed by the Lifelong Kindergarten Group at MIT Media Lab.

Scratch's Building Block Approach to Programming

Scratch is a new programming language, initially released in March 2006. Scratch is different from other programming languages like Visual Basic in that it does not support a text-based approach to programming, as demonstrated here:

```
//Excerpt from a Visual Basic application
If strCurrentAction = "FillCircle" Then
    Dim objCoordinates As Rectangle
        objCoordinates = _
    New Rectangle(Math.Min(objEnd.X, objStart.X), _
    Math.Min(objEnd.Y, objStart.Y), _
    Math.Abs(objEnd.X - objStart.X), _
    Math.Abs(objEnd.Y - objStart.Y))
    Pick_Color_And_Draw("FillCircle", objCoordinates)
End If
```

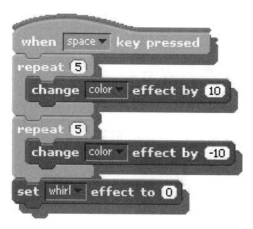

Figure 1.1
An example of how programming logic is outlined in a Scratch application project.

In text-based programming languages, code statements are formulated by following a complex set of syntax rules. Failure to precisely follow these rules when writing statements leads to syntax errors that prevent applications from running. Scratch, on the other hand, uses a different approach. Scratch application projects are built by selecting and snapping together graphical programming blocks, as demonstrated in Figure 1.1.

By using code blocks in place of complex program text statements, Scratch significantly simplifies application development while still making use of the same basic programming logic and concepts implemented in other programming languages. As Figure 1.1 demonstrates, each code block represents a different command or action. Blocks fit together like pieces in a puzzle. You can only snap together blocks in ways that make syntactic sense, completely eliminating syntax errors that proliferate in other programming languages.

Some code blocks are configurable, allowing you to specify things like the number of times an action should execute, text that is to be displayed, or the color to be used when displaying something on the screen. Despite its use of graphical code blocks, Scratch supports the same basic set of programming techniques and constructs as do other traditional programming languages. For example, Scratch supports variables, conditional and iterative logic, and event-driven programming. Scratch also supports the manipulation of graphics and the integration of sound into application projects.

Note

Scratch is designed for teaching first-time programmers how to program. To make the learning experience as straightforward and understandable as possible, the developers of Scratch have sometimes sacrificed programming power and features in favor of simplicity and ease of learning. The goal of the Scratch development team is to promote learning and not to develop a programming language capable of delivering every advanced programming feature required by professional programmers. As a result, Scratch lacks some programming features currently supported in advanced programming languages. Instead, Scratch focuses on fundamental programming concepts to provide new programmers with a foundation upon which they can later build, when and if they decide to move on to other programming languages.

Installing Scratch

Before you can use Scratch, you need to install it on your computer. The installation process varies, depending on whether you use Microsoft Windows or Mac OS X. Instructions for installing Scratch on both of these operating systems are provided in the sections that follow. You will find the installation files needed to install Scratch 1.2.1 on this book's companion CD-ROM. Alternatively, you can download a copy of Scratch from the Scratch website by executing the following steps:

1. Go to http://scratch.mit.edu and click on the Download Scratch Now! link.

2. The Download Scratch page appears. Fill in the optional form to receive updates about Scratch.

3. Click on the Continue to Scratch Download button. The web page shown in Figure 1.2 displays. Click on the appropriate link for your operating system.

The Windows download file is provided as a self-extracting executable named ScratchInstaller.exe. The Mac OS X installation file is provided as a Mac OS X disk image file named MacScratch.dmg. Both of these installation files are approximately 30MB in size, so to download them you will want to use a broadband Internet connection.

Note

There is no official Linux version of Scratch currently available. However, a user-adapted version of Scratch, along with instructions for installing it, is available at http://tcpdpodcast.org/scratch.html.

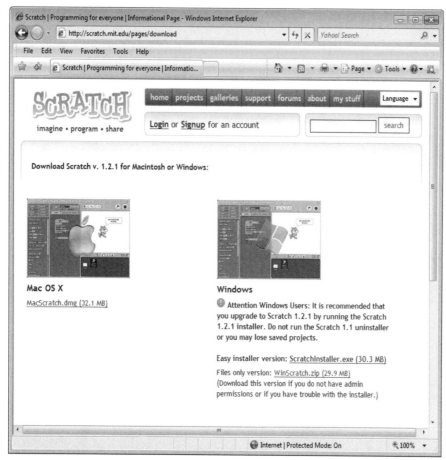

Figure 1.2
Downloading either the Mac OS X or Windows version of Scratch.

Installing Java on Windows

While Mac OS X comes with Java already installed, Windows does not. Fortunately, installing Java on Microsoft Windows is both free and easy. To do so, go to http://java.com/en/download as shown in Figure 1.3 and click on the Free Java Download button.

Once the online installation process begins, you will need to complete the following steps to finish installing Java:

1. After clicking on the Free Java Download button, you may be prompted by a Windows security window for permission to allow the installation process to continue. If so, click on the Continue button.

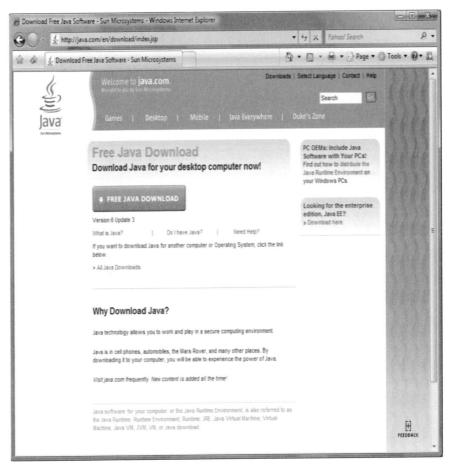

Figure 1.3
Java is required to view and execute Scratch projects loaded onto the Scratch website.

2. Next, a window will appear requesting permission to begin the installation process. Click on the Install button to continue.

3. Finally, a Java Setup Wizard will appear, requiring that you accept the Java License Agreement. Click on the Accept button and then follow the rest of the wizard's instruction to complete the installation process.

Installing Scratch on Windows

Scratch installs on Microsoft Windows like any other Windows application. The following procedure outlines the steps involved in completing Scratch's install process:

Figure 1.4
Installing Scratch on Microsoft Windows.

1. Double-click on the ScratchInstaller.exe file.

2. If prompted for confirmation, click on Run to allow the installation process to begin.

3. If a security message displays, click on Allow to give permission for the installation process to continue.

4. The Scratch Setup Wizard will then appear, as demonstrated in Figure 1.4. Click on Next and follow the instructions provided by the wizard to complete the installation process.

5. Once the Scratch Setup Wizard has completed the installation process, you will need to click on the Finish button to close the wizard. Scratch will then automatically start, as demonstrated in Figure 1.5. In addition, a shortcut for Scratch will be added to the Windows desktop.

Note

In addition to being able to start Scratch by clicking on its desktop shortcut icon, you can click on Start > All Programs > the Scratch folder > and then the Scratch icon.

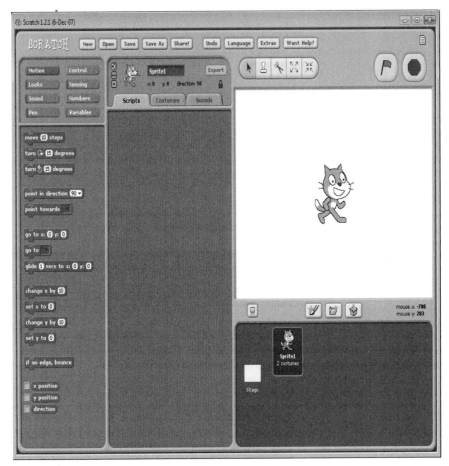

Figure 1.5
Running Scratch on Microsoft Windows Vista.

Installing Scratch on Mac OS X

To install Scratch on Mac OS X, double-click on the MacScratch.dmg archive file to open it. Inside you will see a folder named Scratch. Drag and drop the Scratch folder to your Applications folder (or to any other location that you want) to install it. The contents of the Scratch folder are shown in Figure 1.6.

To start Scratch and begin working with it, double-click on the Scratch icon, which is represented as a cartoon image of a cat. Within a few moments, the Scratch IDE should appear, as shown in Figure 1.7.

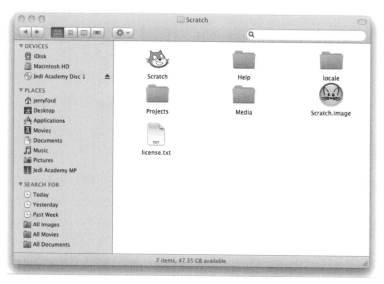

Figure 1.6
Installing Scratch on Mac OS X.

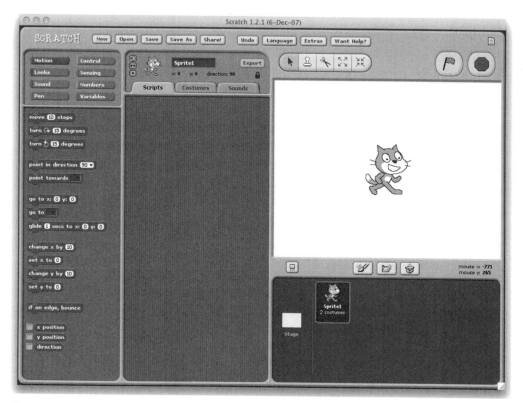

Figure 1.7
Running Scratch on Mac OS X 10.5.

Note

The first time you start Scratch, Mac OS X may display a popup dialog window prompting you for confirmation that you want to run Scratch, because it is an application downloaded from the Internet. Click on the Open button to allow Scratch to start. This popup dialog window will not display upon subsequent startups.

Creating Your First Scratch Application

Scratch application projects are made up of objects called sprites. A *sprite* is a two-dimensional bitmap image drawn on a transparent background. Sprites can be moved around and made to interact with one another. Sprites consist of three primary components, as outlined here:

- **Scripts.** Collections of code blocks that outline the programming logic that controls the operation of sprites.

- **Costumes.** Images that are used to display the sprite on an area of the Scratch IDE, referred to as the stage. Sprites can consist of any number of costumes.

- **Sounds.** Sound effects that are played during application execution when certain events occur or as background audio.

A sprite's appearance can be changed by assigning it different costumes. To move a sprite and control its behavior, you snap together code blocks to create scripts. Sprites can have any number of scripts associated with them. Scripts can be run by double-clicking the code blocks that make them up, in which case each block in the script is executed in top-down order. You can also set things up so that scripts automatically run when various events occur. For example, you can configure script execution to occur when a sprite is clicked or when it interacts with other sprites.

Sprites are displayed and interact with one another on a *stage*. As such, sprites are often referred to as *actors*. Scratch's stage is located in the upper-right corner of its graphical interface.

Note

Sprites can be selected from a predefined collection of graphic objects supplied with Scratch. They can also be copied and pasted from your hard drive or the Internet or created using Scratch's built-in Paint Editor.

Creating a New Scratch Project

Now that you are familiar with the basic components of sprites, let's spend a few minutes learning how to create your first Scratch application project. All new Scratch projects automatically contain a single sprite, representing an image of a kitten. By default, the sprite, named Sprite1, does not have any scripts but does have two costumes and two sounds associated with it. Using this sprite, let's create a Scratch application project that makes the kitten meow and say "Hello World!" when clicked.

The first step in creating a new Scratch application is to click on the New button located at the top of the Scratch IDE. In response, Scratch will create a new project, as shown in Figure 1.8.

As Figure 1.8 shows, the Scratch IDE is organized into a number of separate components. For starters, the code block area contains code blocks, organized into eight different collections. You will use selected code blocks to create a script that makes the kitten talk.

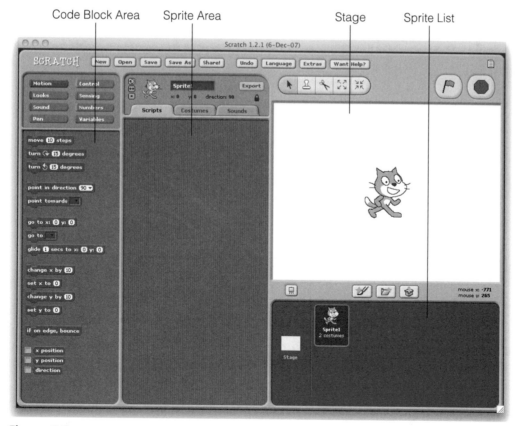

Figure 1.8
Creating a new Scratch application project.

To the right of the code block area is the sprite area. Information about the currently selected sprite is displayed at the top of this area. Just beneath this information are three tabs, which are used to control access to the scripts, costumes, and sounds belonging to the sprite. To the right of the sprite area is the stage, which currently displays the default costume belonging to Sprite1. Just beneath the stage is the sprite list, which displays a list of all the sprites that make up the application project.

Note

Chapter 2, "Getting Comfortable with the Scratch Development Environment," provides a detailed overview of all of the components that make up the Scratch IDE.

Changing Sprite Attributes

The application project that you are creating is designed to work with the default sprite. Rather than use the sprite's default name of Sprite1, let's assign it a more descriptive name. To do so, overtype the text displayed at the top of the sprite area with the word Cat. Once you change the name assigned to the sprite, the name change will automatically be reflected in the sprite list. If you look at the entry for the sprite in the sprite list, you should see a picture of the sprite, its new name, and the number of costumes currently assigned to the sprite (you can click on the Costumes tab at the top of the sprite area to view the sprite's costumes).

Adding Code Blocks

Now that you have changed the name of the sprite, it is time to add the code blocks required to make the cat meow and say "Hello World!" Let's begin by clicking on the Sound button located at the top of the code block area. This displays a collection of code blocks that control the playback of sound effects. Locate the code block labeled play sound and drag and drop it onto the sprite area, as shown in Figure 1.9.

By default, this code block is automatically set up to play an audio file that makes a meow sound. Next, click on the Looks button located at the top of the code block area. This displays a collection of code blocks that control the appearance of a sprite. Locate the code block labeled say Hello! for 2 secs and drag and drop it onto the sprite area, as shown in Figure 1.10.

By default, this code block displays a text string inside a graphical bubble caption. This code block has two editable fields: a text field and a numeric field. Since the

Figure 1.9
Using a sound block to make the kitten meow.

kitten is supposed to display the message "Hello world!" when clicked, replace the text "Hello!" with "Hello World!".

As previously stated, you can run a script at any time by double-clicking on it. To test this, double-click on one of the two code blocks that you have added and then watch the kitten on the stage, and you'll hear it meow and display its message. Rather than having to double-click on the script to make the kitten do its thing, let's set things up so that the kitten automatically meows and talks whenever you click on it. This is accomplished by clicking on the Control button located at the top of the code block area and then dragging and dropping the control block labeled when Cat clicked on top of the two buttons you have already added to the sprite's script, as demonstrated in Figure 1.11.

The when Cat clicked block automatically snaps in place as you move it toward the top of the script. With this block now in place, click on the script file and see

Figure 1.10
Using a looks block to make the kitten say something.

what happens. As demonstrated in Figure 1.12, the kitten responds by meowing and talking (displaying "Hello world!" in a text caption bubble).

Saving Your Work

Okay, now that you have your new Scratch application project working, it is time to save your work. This is done by clicking on the Save button located at the top of the Scratch IDE. In response, the Save Project window shown in Figure 1.13 displays, allowing you to assign a name to your project and store it on your computer.

Type **Hello World** in the New Filename field to name your application. If you want, you can type your name in the Project Author field and then enter a short description in the About This Project field and then click on the OK button to save your project.

Figure 1.11
Using a control block to control script execution.

That's it. At this point, you have gone through all of the steps necessary to create, test, modify, execute, and then save a new Scratch application project. Now that wasn't too tough, was it? Before wrapping up this chapter, let's spend a few minutes learning about Scratch's global community of users and how you can tap in to learn more about Scratch.

Joining Scratch's Global Community

Scratch is supported by a global community of students, teachers, schools, parents, and computer enthusiasts and hobbyists. Scratch is available in many languages, including English, Spanish, German, French, Italian, Hungarian, Hebrew, Polish, Dutch, Romanian, and Russian. The Scratch website, located at http://scratch.mit.edu and shown in Figure 1.14, helps bring together people from around the world and facilitates the development of the Scratch community.

Figure 1.12
Automating a sprite with a script.

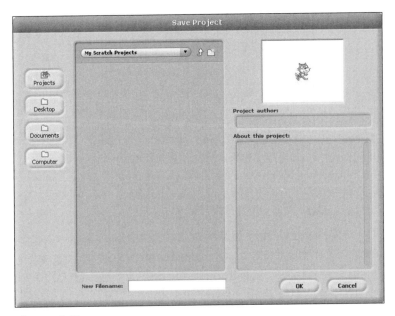

Figure 1.13
Saving your new Scratch application project.

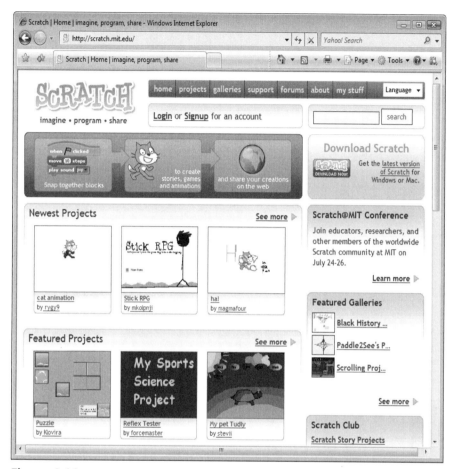

Figure 1.14
The Scratch website is the linchpin supporting the growth and interaction of the Scratch community.

The Scratch website provides access to all kinds of resources that help Scratch programmers learn more about the language. It provides access to online documentation and training videos. It also provides access to the help screen packed with documentation on how to work with Scratch code blocks.

Sharing Your Application Projects

The Scratch website promotes application project sharing by allowing Scratch programmers to upload their projects and make them available to anyone visiting the website. This allows Scratch programmers to show off their work and to learn from the work of others. In fact, every Scratch project that is uploaded to the website can be downloaded and used as the basis for creating new projects. As

Figure 1.15
The Scratch website facilitates sharing by promoting Scratch projects and making them available for download.

Figure 1.15 shows, the Scratch website actively promotes Scratch applications on its project page (http://scratch.mit.edu/channel/recent), which means that you can expect to see any Scratch projects that you upload posted there as well.

The Scratch website lets members post their uploaded Scratch projects in galleries. You can post your Scratch projects in different galleries or create a gallery of your own and even control whether anyone else is allowed to upload their projects into it. As Figure 1.16 demonstrates, the Scratch website actively promotes member galleries.

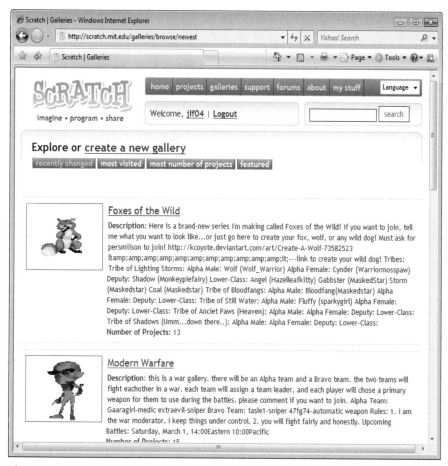

Figure 1.16
You can create your own gallery and use it to promote your programming skills.

If you decide to create your own gallery, you can customize it by assigning it a name and a description and by determining whether you want to let anyone else upload Scratch projects into it.

Registering with the Scratch Website

In order to upload your Scratch projects to the Scratch website, you must sign up for a free account, which you can do by clicking on the sign up link at the top of every page on the Scratch website. Clicking on this link opens the Create an Account page, shown in Figure 1.17.

The Scratch website gives its members the ability to comment on any Scratch application project that is uploaded to the website. The website also provides

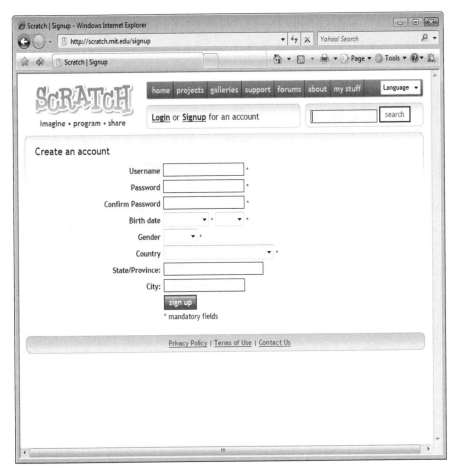

Figure 1.17
Registering for a free account on the Scratch website.

access to a collection of forums designed to host conversation between students, teachers, and Scratch enthusiasts from all over the world.

Note

You will learn more about how to share your Scratch projects when you get to Chapter 13, "Sharing Your Scratch Projects Over the Internet."

Keeping In Touch

In addition to facilitating project sharing and allowing comments to be posted about projects, the Scratch website hosts a number of online forums at http://scratch.mit.edu/forums/, as shown in Figure 1.18.

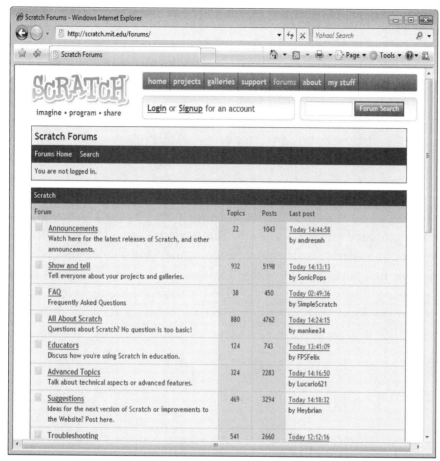

Figure 1.18
Members of the Scratch community can communicate freely and discuss ideas using the forums hosted on the Scratch website.

As Figure 1.18 shows, forums have been set up to address the following range of topics:

- Announcements

- Show and tell

- FAQ

- All About Scratch

- Educators

- Advanced Topics

- Suggestions

- Troubleshooting

These forums provide the ability to learn directly from other Scratch programmers. By reading the discussions that are posted, you can learn new programming techniques and find out about problems encountered by other programmers and their solutions. Most important of all, you can post questions and get answers to those questions.

Summary

This chapter has provided an overview of the Scratch language and it capabilities. It showed you how to install Scratch on your computer and then demonstrated how to create your first Scratch application. It also introduced you to the Scratch website and explained the importance of setting up an account and becoming an active member of the Scratch community.

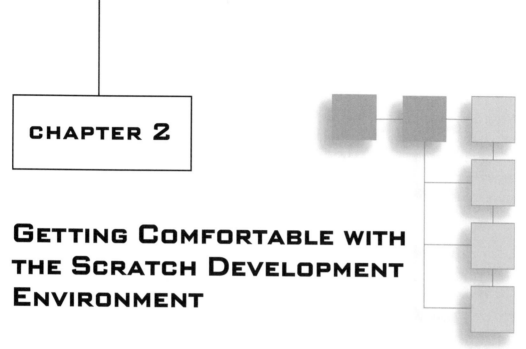

CHAPTER 2

GETTING COMFORTABLE WITH THE SCRATCH DEVELOPMENT ENVIRONMENT

To become an effective Scratch programmer, you need to become intimately familiar with its integrated development environment, or IDE. In this chapter, you will learn about the stage on which applications execute and the sprite list that Scratch uses to display and organize sprites used in your applications. You will also learn how to work with editors that create scripts, costumes, and sound effects. You will also learn all about Scratch's paint program, which you can use to create your own custom graphics files. By the time you have completed this chapter, you will have a solid understanding of all of the features and capabilities of the Scratch IDE and will be ready to begin using it to create your own Scratch application projects.

An overview of the major topics covered in this chapter includes:

- How to work with menu and toolbar buttons

- How to add, remove, and modify the sprites that make up your Scratch applications

- An explanation of the coordinates system used to control sprite placements on the stage

- How to edit and modify scripts, costumes, and sounds

- How to create new sprites using Scratch's built-in Paint Editor

Getting Comfortable with the Scratch IDE

Scratch is a graphical programming language. Scratch applications are created by executing Scratch projects made up of different types of media, including graphics and sound, using scripts made up of different code blocks. Scratch projects are created using its IDE. As shown in Figure 2.1, Scratch's IDE is composed of numerous components.

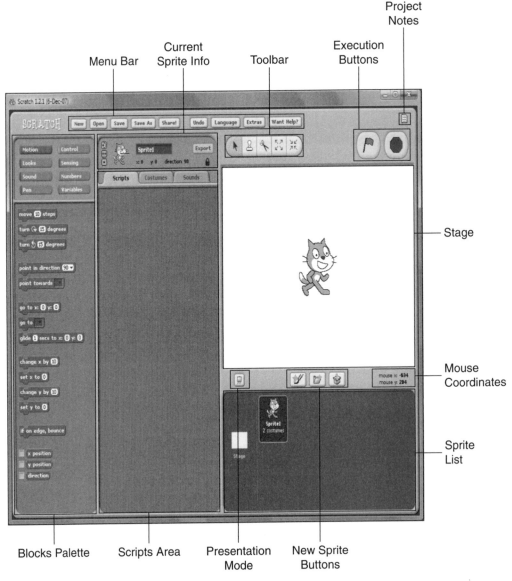

Figure 2.1
The Scratch IDE facilitates the development and execution of Scratch applications.

Together, all of the components identified in Figure 2.1 provide a robust and powerful, yet initiative and fun, work environment, providing everything needed to develop Scratch applications. The rest of this chapter will offer a detailed overview of each of the major components that make up the Scratch IDE.

Getting Familiar with Menu Bar Commands

Like most graphic applications, the Scratch IDE has a menu bar made up of a collection of buttons located at the top of the IDE, as shown in Figure 2.2.

These buttons provide access to commands that allow you to create, open, and save Scratch projects as well as share them on the Internet, undo previous commands, change the language used by the IDE, and much more. The following list provides an explanation of each of the buttons that make up the menu bar.

- **New.** Creates a new Scratch application project.

- **Open.** Opens an existing Scratch application project.

- **Save.** Saves the current Scratch project (with a file extension of .sb).

- **Save As.** Saves the current Scratch project under a new name.

- **Share!** Uploads a copy of the project to the Scratch website (http://scratch .mit.edu) where it can be made available for viewing and downloaded by other Scratch programmers.

- **Undo.** Restores the last script, code block, or sprite deleted from the application project during the current working session.

- **Language.** Lets you specify the language to be used by the Scratch IDE.

- **Extras.** Displays a popup list from which you can select one of the following commands: `Import Project`, `Start Single Stepping`, `Compress Sounds`, or `Compress Images`.

Figure 2.2
The menu bar provides easy access to commands that you can use to create and save Scratch projects.

■ **Want Help?** Displays a page that provides a link to the Scratch website as well as to the following set of resources: Reference Materials, Tutorials, or Frequently Asked Questions.

Most of the commands listed above are self-explanatory. However, the last three commands merit additional explanation. When clicked, the Language button displays a menu of programming languages from which you can select. Depending on the language selected, a complete translation may be available. In other cases, only scripts and code blocks may be translated.

Tip

You can display a tool tip for any of the button controls shown on the Scratch IDE by moving the mouse pointer over the button.

When clicked, the Extras button displays a menu that has the following options.

■ **About.** Displays a popup window that provides information about the version of Scratch being used.

■ **Import Project.** This command imports all of the sprites and backgrounds, along with any related scripts, from the specified project into the current project. As such, this command makes the sharing and movement of sprites and backgrounds between Scratch projects a snap.

■ **Start Single Stepping.** This command tells Scratch to execute an application a step at a time, allowing you to observe the execution flow of code blocks. This command will be discussed more thoroughly in Chapter 15, "Finding and Fixing Program Errors."

■ **Compress Sounds.** This command compresses any sound files used by the current application project to reduce the project's size. This is important because the Scratch website imposes a 10MB limit on the size of Scratch applications.

■ **Compress Images.** Like the Compress Sounds command, this command compresses any graphic image files used by the current application project to reduce the project's size. By compressing the size of your application, you can sometimes reduce large Scratch projects enough to allow them to upload.

The last button on Scratch's menu bar is the Want Help? button. When clicked, this button opens a browser window that provides access to the following resources.

- **Getting Started.** Opens the "Getting Started with Scratch" PDF user guide.

- **Help Screens.** Displays a collection of help screens that document the use and purpose of every Scratch code block.

- **Reference Guide.** Opens the Scratch "Reference Guide" PDF reference file.

- **Visit the Scratch support page.** Displays the Scratch support web page located at http://scratch.wik.is/Support.

Running Scratch Applications on the Stage

The stage is the area on the Scratch IDE, located in the upper-right side, as shown in Figure 2.3, where your Scratch applications execute. The stage provides a place for the sprites that make up your applications to interact with one another and the user.

Figure 2.3
The stage provides the canvas upon which sprites are displayed and interact with one another.

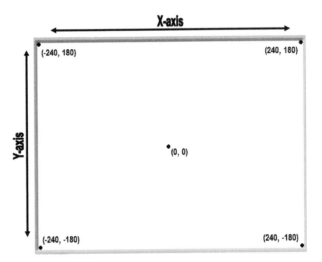

Figure 2.4
Sprites are placed on the screen and moved around using a system of coordinates.

The stage is 480 units wide and 360 units high. The stage is mapped out into a logical grid using a coordinate system made up of an X-axis and a Y-axis, as demonstrated in Figure 2.4.

As you can see, the X-axis runs from coordinates 240 to –240, and the Y-axis coordinate runs from coordinates 180 to –180. The middle of the stage has a coordinate location of (0, 0). Scratch keeps you informed of the pointer's location whenever it is moved over the stage by displaying its (X, Y) coordinate position in the mouse x: and mouse y: fields just beneath the bottom-right side of the stage.

The stage can be assigned one or more backgrounds, allowing you to change its appearance during application execution. By default, all Scratch applications are assigned a blank background. You can add new backgrounds by clicking on the Stage thumbnail, located on the left-hand side of the sprite list, and then clicking on the Backgrounds tab located just above the scripts area. Like sprites, the stage can be assigned its own scripts and sound effects.

Tip

If you right-click on an open area on the stage, a popup menu will appear, displaying the following menu items:

- **Grab screen region for new sprite.** Makes a copy of a selected portion of the stage and uses it to create a new sprite.

- **Save picture of stage.** Saves a copy of the stage as a .GIF file.

Running Applications in Presentation Mode

As you saw in Chapter 1 when you created the Hello World project, Scratch runs your applications on the stage within the IDE by default. However, if you click on the Presentation Mode button, located just beneath the bottom-left corner of the stage, you can run your Scratch application project in Presentation mode. To see how this works, click on the Open button located at the top of the Scratch IDE and then locate and open the Hello World project. Next, click on the Presentation Mode button to switch to full-screen mode. Once in Presentation screen mode, single-click on the sprite representing the kitten and watch as your application executes, as demonstrated in Figure 2.5.

You can exit Presentation mode at any time either by clicking on the Exit Presentation Mode icon located just above the upper-left side of the stage or by pressing the Escape key.

Controlling Application Execution

Whether running your application from the IDE's stage or in Presentation mode, you can automatically start any scripts that begin with the green flag control block by clicking on the green flag button located in the upper-right corner of the IDE, as shown in Figure 2.6. This same button is also available in Presentation mode. By clicking on the red stop button located right next to the green flag

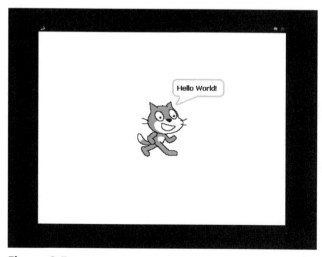

Figure 2.5
Running a Scratch application project in Presentation mode.

Figure 2.6
The green flag and red stop buttons provide control over script execution.

button, you can stop the execution of your applications any time you finish working with them.

Working with the Sprite List

Scratch applications are made up of sprites that interact with one another as they move around the stage. Each sprite that makes up a Scratch application is displayed as a thumbnail in the sprite list area, located on the lower-right portion of the Scratch IDE, as shown in Figure 2.7. Although it has no impact on a Scratch application, you can reorganize the order in which sprites are displayed in the sprite list by dragging and dropping thumbnails to any location that makes sense to you.

In addition to a thumbnail, Scratch also displays the name of each sprite as well as the number of scripts and costumes belonging to each sprite. To work with a sprite and edit its scripts, costumes, and sound effects, just click on its thumbnail. The currently selected sprite is highlighted by a blue outline. Once selected, you can click on the Scripts, Costumes, and Sounds tabs located at the top of the script area to edit a sprite's scripts, costumes, and sound effects.

Figure 2.7
The sprite list displays a thumbnail for each sprite in an application.

If you right-click on a sprite's thumbnail, the following list of menu options is displayed:

- **Show.** Centers a sprite on the stage, placing it on top of all other sprites.

- **Export this sprite.** Exports a sprite as a file, making it available to be imported into other Scratch projects.

- **Duplicate.** Makes a copy of the sprite.

- **Delete.** Removes a sprite from the project.

Tip

You can also export, duplicate, and delete sprites by right-clicking on any sprite on the stage and then selecting the corresponding menu items that are displayed.

The sprite list also displays a thumbnail representing the application project's stage. When the stage's thumbnail is selected, you can add scripts to the stage, modify the stage's background by assigning it one or more graphic files, and also add sounds to the stage.

Generating New Sprites

Scratch makes it easy for you to work with sprites by providing three different options for adding them to your applications. These options are accessed through the New Sprite buttons located just below the stage, as shown in Figure 2.8.

When clicked, the Paint New Sprite button starts Scratch's Paint Editor program. This program provides everything you need to draw new sprites on a transparent

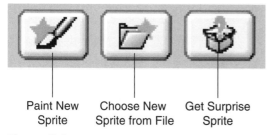

Paint New   Choose New   Get Surprise
Sprite   Sprite from File   Sprite

Figure 2.8
The New Sprite buttons provide access to tools for adding and creating new sprites.

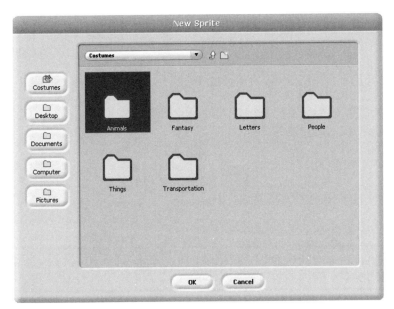

Figure 2.9
Scratch supplies easy access to a wide selection of ready-made sprites.

background. You will learn the ins and outs of how to work with the Paint Editor program a little later in this chapter.

When clicked, the Choose New Sprite from File button displays the New Sprite window shown in Figure 2.9, providing access to different collections of graphic files that you can add to your Scratch applications as sprites. To select and add a sprite, all you have to do is to drill down into one of Scratch's folders, find the sprite you want, and then click on the OK button. The sprite that you selected will then appear in the center of the stage, and a thumbnail representing the sprite will be added to the sprite list.

The Get Surprise Sprite button randomly retrieves one of Scratch's ready-made sprites and adds it to your application project. It can be used to generate all kinds of wacky projects.

Tracking Mouse Pointer Location

As you learn how to develop your own Scratch applications, you will need to keep track of the initial placement and subsequent movement of sprites on the stage. Scratch assists you in this task by keeping track of mouse-pointer movement whenever you move the pointer across the stage (see Figure 2.10). You can use

mouse x: **-49**

mouse y: **43**

Figure 2.10
The Scratch IDE makes it easy to track the mouse-pointer's location when it moves around the stage.

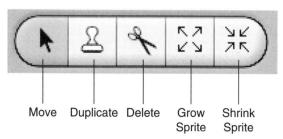

Move   Duplicate   Delete   Grow   Shrink
                            Sprite Sprite

Figure 2.11
The Scratch toolbar provides tools for interacting with sprites.

this information to identify the coordinates data that you need to incorporate into your application code as you develop the programming logic that drives your Scratch projects.

Working with the Scratch Toolbar

Another important component of the Scratch IDE is the toolbar, shown in Figure Figure 2.11. The toolbar provides access to commands that you can use to interact with and control the sprites that make up your applications.

The following list summarizes the functionality provided by each of the toolbar's buttons:

- **Move.** Allows you to drag and drop sprites to different locations on the stage (default toolbar selection).

- **Duplicate.** Makes a copy of the currently selected sprite, including its scripts, costumes, and sounds, providing an easy way of adding new sprites to your applications. Once a sprite is duplicated, you can customize the new copy of the sprite as you see fit.

- **Delete.** Removes a sprite, including all its scripts, costumes, and sounds, from the project and removes its thumbnail from the sprite list.

- **Grow Sprite.** Increases a sprite's size, in case its actual size does not meet the needs of your application.

- **Shrink Sprite.** Decreases a sprite's size, in case its actual size does not meet the needs of your application.

By default, the Move button is always selected. However, you may select any of the other toolbar buttons by clicking on them and then clicking on the sprite that you want to work with.

Switching Between Code Block Groups

Like applications created by any programming language, Scratch applications execute program code made up of collections of code blocks that manipulate sprites and interact with the user. Scratch's program code is organized into scripts belonging to sprites. Every sprite in an application can be assigned one or more scripts. In addition, the stage can also execute its own scripts.

As you have already seen, the first step in creating a script is to select the sprite (or the stage) to which the script will belong. This is done by clicking on the appropriate thumbnail in the sprites list. You can then add code blocks by dragging the blocks from the blocks palette and dropping them into the scripts area (when the Script tab is selected). The blocks palette is organized into two sections. The top section contains eight button controls, each of which represents a different category of code block. Each of the buttons is color coded. The currently selected button is easily identified because it is filled in with its assigned color. The left-hand edge of the unselected buttons shows the color of the code blocks belonging to its category. For example, Figure 2.12 shows how the blocks palette looks when the Motion button has been selected.

Trick

You can right-click (Control-click on Mac OS X) on any code block and then select Help from the resulting popup menu to get help information on any code block.

Getting Comfortable with the Scripts Area

The last major part of the Scratch IDE that you need to become familiar with is the scripts area, which consists of two major sections. The Current Sprite Info section, located at the top of the scripts area, displays information about the currently selected sprite. The rest of the scripts area is controlled by three tabs, which allow you to add scripts, costumes, and sounds to sprites.

Figure 2.12
Each category of code block is designed to accomplish a related set of tasks.

Figure 2.13
Changing a sprite's name and viewing detailed information about the sprite.

Examining Sprite Details

The Current Sprite Info section displays the name currently assigned to the selected sprite, which, as demonstrated in Figure 2.13, is Sprite1. You can change a sprite's name by typing over it. The sprite's current coordinates and direction are displayed just beneath its name, and the sprite's currently assigned costume is displayed just to the left of its name.

Figure 2.14
Exporting a sprite as a stand-alone graphic file.

Take note of the blue line that is displayed on the thumbnail in the Current Sprite Info section. It shows the sprite's currently assigned direction. You can change the sprite's direction by dragging the outside edge of this line to a new direction. If you do not like the direction that you have set for the sprite, double-click on the sprite to reset it back to its default direction (90-degree angle).

You can export the scripts as a stand-alone line by clicking on the Export button. This opens the Export Sprite window shown in Figure 2.14, allowing you to specify the location where you want to save the sprite, making it available for use in other Scratch application projects.

Just beneath the Export button is a graphic file representing a padlock. Clicking on this image toggles the graphic between a locked and unlocked state. When set to locked, Scratch prevents the sprite from being dragged around the stage by the user when the script is run in Presentation mode or when run from the Scratch website.

Just to the left of the sprite's currently selected costume are three buttons that you can use to specify the sprite's rotation style. These three buttons are mutually exclusive, meaning that you can only select one. Table 2.1 identifies the rotational style represented by each of these buttons.

Table 2.1 Sprite Rotational Buttons

Button	Name	Description
	Can rotate	Rotates the sprite's costume by 360 degree when the sprite's direction is changed.
	Only face left-right	Toggles the direction that the sprite's costume faces from left to right and vice versa.
	Don't rotate	Maintains the sprite costume's current direction.

Tip

To get a better feel of the effect that Scratch's rotational buttons have on a sprite, click on each of them and observe the rotational movement of the sprite costume in the Current Sprite Info section.

Editing Scripts

As you have already seen, Scratch scripts are created by dragging code blocks from the blocks palette onto the scripts area (when the Scripts tab has been selected). Of course, the code blocks must be added in a manner that makes logical sense, which is what Chapters 5 through 22 are designed to teach you.

Tip

As you add new scripts and modify existing ones, it is easy to leave the scripts area in a mess. One way of dealing with this situation it to spend a few minutes dragging and dropping scripts so that they line up and are evenly spaced. However, a much faster and easier option is to right-click on a free area within the scripts area and then click on the clean-up option located in the popup menu that is displayed. In response, Scratch will realign all of your scripts for you.

Adding Costumes

A sprite can have one or more costumes, allowing it to change its appearance as an application executes. A sprite must have at least one costume. For example, Figure 2.15 shows a sprite that has two costumes. Each costume is assigned a unique name and number (displayed just to the left of the costume's image).

By default, Scratch only displays a sprite's first costume. You can drag and drop costumes to change their position in the list. When moved, the number assigned to the costume is automatically changed as well.

Scratch gives you three different ways of adding new costumes to sprites. For starters, you can click on the Paint button. This opens the Paint Editor program,

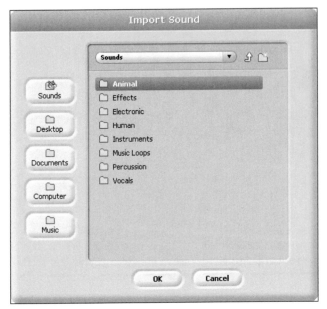

Figure 2.15
Importing and assigning a sound file to a sprite.

which you can use to draw a new costume. You can also add a new costume to a sprite by clicking on the Import button and specifying an image file from a folder on your computer. Lastly, you can drag and drop an image file from the Internet or your desktop onto the scripts area when the Costumes tab is selected.

Note

Scratch can work with different types of graphic files, including GIF, JPG, BMP, and PNG files. Scratch can also work with animated GIF files. An *animated GIF* file is a graphic made up of two or more frames, each of which is displayed as an automated sequence when the GIF file is displayed.

Once added, you can modify a costume by selecting it and clicking on the Edit button, which opens the Paint Editor. You can also add a new costume to a sprite by selecting an existing costume and then clicking on the Copy button. Once the copy of the costume has been added, you can click on its Edit button, allowing you to modify it using the Paint Editor.

You can delete a costume from a sprite by selecting it and then clicking on the round Delete button to the right of the Copy button. You can also turn a costume into a sprite or export it as a stand-alone costume by right-clicking on it and selecting the appropriate option from the popup menu that appears.

Note

The stage can be assigned a graphic to be used as a background upon which the application's sprites are displayed. In fact, the stage can be assigned a series of backgrounds, allowing an application to change backgrounds during application execution. To view, edit, and make a copy of a background, select the stage thumbnail located in the sprite list. When you do this, the Costumes tab in the scripts area changes to the Backgrounds tab, allowing you to modify and work with application backgrounds. From here you can also create new backgrounds yourself by clicking on the Paint button. This opens Scratch's Paint Editor program, discussed later in this chapter, allowing you to create any background you want. You can also click on the Import button to add an external graphic file to your application as a background.

Adding Sound Effects

Just as sprites can have different costumes, you can also assign one or more sounds to them (or to the stage), which can be played during application execution, either as background music or noise or as sound effects during game play. Scratch can play back MP3 files as well as most WAV, AU, and AIF audio files. To view the sound files associated with a sprite or to record or import a new file, select the sprite's thumbnail in the sprite list and then click on the Sounds tab in the scripts area. A list of the sound files belonging to the sprite is displayed, as demonstrated in Figure 2.16.

Figure 2.16
Adding and editing sound files.

Once the Sounds tab has been selected, you can perform any of the following actions on any sound files that belong to the sprite:

- Change the name used to refer to the sound within the application.

- Click on the Play button to listen to the sound.

- Click on the Stop button to halt sound playback.

- Click on the Delete button to remove the sound from the application project.

In addition to interacting with a sprite's existing sound file, you may add new sound files by clicking on the Record button. In response, the Sound Recorder window appears, as shown in Figure 2.17, allowing you to record and save a new sound file. Of course, to record your own sound files, your computer will need to have a microphone.

You can also add new sound files to your Scratch application by clicking on the Import button, which opens the Import Sound window, as shown in Figure 2.18, allowing you to select a sound file. Scratch provides access to tons of prerecorded sound files. By default, the Import Sound window displays a listing of folders containing different collections of sound files.

Keeping Project Notes

Another important feature of the Scratch IDE is the ability to add and update project notes. Scratch allows you to add project notes when you first save your application project. Once they are saved, you may update your project's notes at any time by clicking on the Project Notes icon located in the upper-right corner of the IDE. In response, the Project Notes window displays, as demonstrated in Figure 2.19.

Figure 2.17
Recording a new audio file to be used as part of a Scratch application.

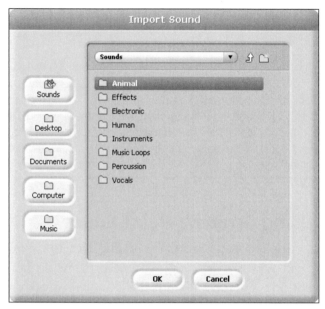

Figure 2.18
Importing and assigning a sound file to a sprite.

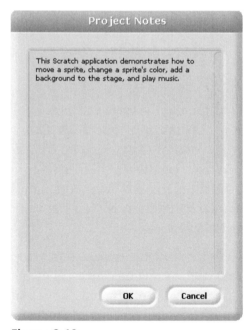

Figure 2.19
Viewing and updating Scratch application project notes.

The Project Notes window operates like a simple Notepad program, allowing you to type in any text you want.

Tip

Use the Project Notes window to help document your Scratch applications, leaving behind information that explains the application's purpose and why you designed it the way you did. If you plan on uploading your project to the Scratch website, then project notes take on additional value. Specifically, text saved as notes is displayed on the same web page as your project and can therefore provide instructions for running your application.

Creating New Sprites Using Scratch's Paint Editor

In addition to using the sprites supplied with Scratch and graphics that you acquire from the Internet, you can always create your own sprite using any graphic/paint program. Although it does not have all of the bells and whistles that applications like Corel Paint Shop Pro or Adobe Photoshop have, Scratch's built-in Paint Editor, shown in Figure 2.20, offers everything needed to draw or modify graphics for use as sprites and backgrounds.

As Figure 2.20 demonstrates, Scratch's Paint Editor is divided into multiple components. Thanks to Scratch's cross-platform design, the Paint Editor looks and operates identically on both Microsoft Windows and Mac OS X.

Examining the Drawing Canvas

Links to the Paint Editor program are located just under the stage and within the Costumes and Backgrounds tabs located in the scripts area. The Paint Editor program can be used to create or modify new sprites, costumes, and backgrounds. Most of the space on the Paint Editor's window is dedicated to a drawing canvas. To draw on the canvas, you select different drawing commands from the toolbar and then use the mouse to draw on the canvas. You can work with different colors and apply a range of special effects.

If the size of the graphic being worked on exceeds the available area, scrollbars are enabled on the right-hand side and the bottom of the drawing canvas, allowing you to view all parts of the graphic. You can also use the Zoom In and Zoom Out buttons located at the bottom of the Paint Editor window to temporarily increase or decrease the magnification of the drawing canvas.

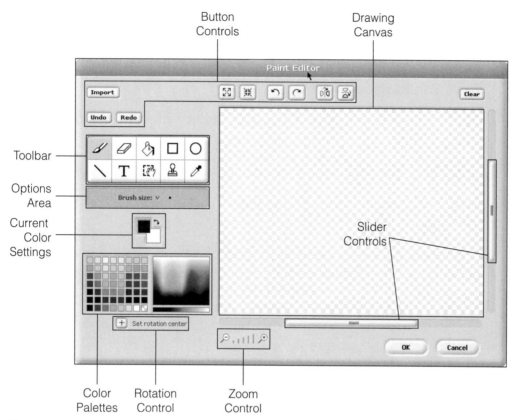

Figure 2.20
Scratch's built-in Paint Editor program provides everything needed to create sprites and costumes.

Working with the Toolbar and Options Area

When creating or editing a graphic image on the drawing canvas, the buttons located on the Paint Editor's toolbar provide access to essential features and functionality. The following list offers an overview of the functionality provided by each toolbar button:

- **Paintbrush.** Allows you to draw freehand on the drawing canvas using the current foreground color and brush size.

- **Eraser.** Allows you to erase selected portions of the drawing canvas using the current eraser size. Erased portions of the drawing canvas are returned to a transparent state.

- **Fill.** Allows you to fill in enclosed areas with either a gradient or a solid color, depending on the selected option specified in the options area.

- **Rectangle.** Allows you to draw filled-in or outlined rectangle shapes using the current foreground color.

- **Ellipse.** Allows you to draw filled-in or outlined ellipses using the current foreground color.

- **Line.** Allows you to draw straight lines using the current foreground color.

- **Text.** Allows you to include text as part of a drawing using the current font type and size.

- **Selection.** Allows you to select a rectangular portion of the drawing canvas and move it to a different part of the drawing canvas (cut and paste).

- **Stamp.** Allows you to select a rectangular portion of the drawing canvas and copy it to different parts of the drawing canvas (copy and paste).

- **Eyedropper.** Allows you to select the foreground color.

Most of the toolbar buttons accept configuration options that further refine the functionality provided by the button control. For example, Figure 2.21 shows the four configuration options that are provided when the Fill button has been selected. These options set the fill style that is applied and include the application of a solid color and the use of a horizontal gradient, vertical gradient, or radial gradient.

Note

A *gradient* is a color created by blending together the foreground and background colors.

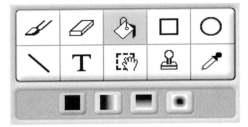

Figure 2.21
The content of the options area changes based on the selected toolbar button.

Working with Button Controls

As shown in Figure 2.22, Scratch's Paint Editor program includes a number of button controls that can initiate an assortment of different actions.

The following list identifies each of these buttons and explains its purpose:

- **Import.** Opens an image from a graphic file stored on your computer.

- **Grow.** Increases the size of the drawing canvas, allowing you to focus in on a particular area.

- **Shrink.** Decreases the size of the drawing canvas.

- **Rotate counterclockwise.** Rotates the drawing canvas counterclockwise.

- **Rotate clockwise.** Rotates the Drawing canvas clockwise.

- **Flip horizontally.** Flips the drawing canvas horizontally.

- **Flip vertically.** Flips the drawing canvas vertically.

- **Clear canvas.** Clears any graphics currently displayed on the drawing canvas.

- **Undo.** Undoes the last action that you performed in the Paint Editor.

- **Redo.** Redoes the last undone action.

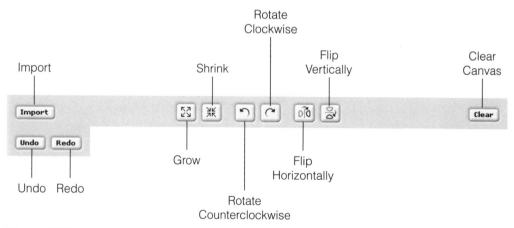

Figure 2.22
The Paint Editor provides access to key functionality through various button controls.

Specifying Color Settings

The Paint Editor lets you specify current color settings for both foreground and background drawing using the current Color Settings control located on the left-hand side of the Paint Editor window, just under the options area. To set the current foreground color, click on the top square and then select a color from one of the color palettes that are displayed beneath the control. Likewise, you can set the current background color by selecting the bottom square and then selecting a color from one of the color palettes.

Configuring a Sprite's Rotation Center

One final but very important Paint Editor feature that you definitely need to know how to use is the Set Rotation Center button located in the lower-left corner of the Paint Editor window. When clicked, this button displays a set of cross-hairs on the Paint Editor's drawing canvas, as demonstrated in Figure 2.23. You can then use drag and drop to move the cross-hair over the portion of the sprite that you want to set up as the sprite's rotational center when the sprite is rotated on the stage.

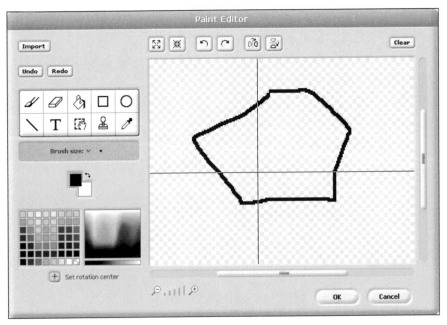

Figure 2.23
Cross-hairs make it easy to set a sprite's rotational center.

The sprite shown in Figure 2.23 is that of a rock that might be used in a space shooter game like *Asteroids*. In this type of game, the asteroid would move around the screen, threatening to destroy the player's ship by colliding with it. To provide a realistic look and feel, you might want to tell Scratch to rotate the rock as its moves around the screen. By setting up the rock's rotation point as the center of the sprite, it will appear to rotate or spin around its center. On the other hand, by settings its rotation point to be one of the edges of the rock, you can make it rotate in a more wobbly manner.

Summary

This chapter has introduced you to the Scratch IDE and provided a step-by-step overview of all of its major components and functionality. You learned how to work with its menu and toolbar buttons. You learned how to add and delete sprites as well as how to add scripts, costumes, and sounds to sprites. This chapter explained the coordinates system used to control the placement of sprites on the stage. On top of all this, this chapter also provided an overview of Scratch's Paint Editor program and outlined all of its major features and functionality.

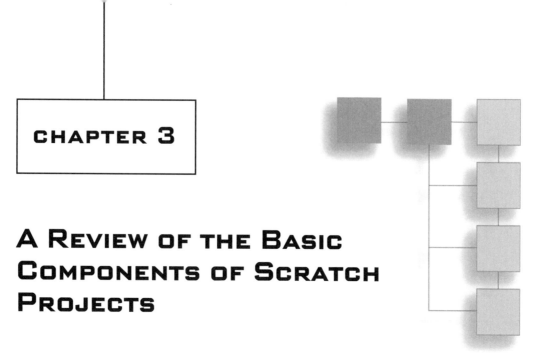

CHAPTER 3

A REVIEW OF THE BASIC COMPONENTS OF SCRATCH PROJECTS

As you have already seen, Scratch application projects are comprised of backgrounds and sprites. Sprites interact and move about the stage under the programmatic control of scripts made up of code blocks. This chapter will explain the three basic types of code blocks and how they work together to create scripts. It will also review the eight categories into which all Scratch's 100-plus code blocks are grouped. Although this chapter does not offer an in-depth review of each individual code block, it will provide a series of tables that you can bookmark and use as a quick reference when developing new Scratch applications.

An overview of the major topics covered in this chapter includes:

- A detailed explanation of stack blocks, hat blocks, and reporter blocks

- A demonstration of how to work with and configure monitors

- A review of all 100-plus code blocks that make up Scratch scripts

- An explanation of how to display help information for individual code blocks

Working with Blocks and Stacks

To bring the backgrounds and sprites that make up Scratch applications to life, you must create scripts. Scripts are created by dragging and dropping code blocks from the blocks palette to the scripts area and snapping them together, creating

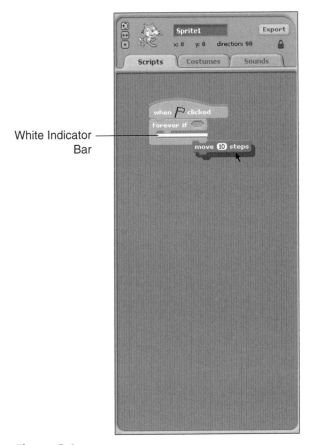

White Indicator
Bar

Figure 3.1
Use the visual indicator to determine valid connection points.

stacks. Scripts can be run by double-clicking on one of the code blocks. Scripts can also be configured to automatically execute when predefined events occur.

You can drag a code block around the scripts area. As demonstrated in Figure 3.1, when you drag a block near other blocks, a white indicator bar appears to designate locations where a valid connection can be made. Code blocks can be snapped to the top and bottom of stacks or inserted into the middle of the stack.

You can move code stacks by clicking on their uppermost blocks and dragging them to a new location. If you drag a block from the middle of a stack, all of the code blocks underneath it are dragged out as well.

Tip

You can copy a stack of code blocks from one sprite to another by dragging and dropping the stack onto the thumbnail of a sprite located in the sprite list.

Three Basic Types of Scratch Blocks

Scratch applications are made up of sprites that interact with one another and the user. Sprites are controlled and animated by scripts. Sprites can have any number of scripts, each of which is designed to perform a specific task or action. Scripts are made up of one of more Scratch code blocks. In total, there are more than 100 different Scratch blocks, each of which is designed to fulfill a specific purpose. These blocks can be broadly classified into three categories, as outlined here:

- Stack blocks
- Hat blocks
- Reporter blocks

Working with Stack Blocks

The majority of code blocks provided by Scratch are stack blocks. *Stack blocks* are code blocks with a notch at the top or a bump at the bottom. The notches and bumps serve as visual indicators that identify how the blocks can be snapped together to create programming logic. Figure 3.2 shows an example of a typical stack block.

The notch on the top indicates that the code block can be attached to the underside of another code block. The bump at the bottom of the code block allows other code blocks to attach to its underside. Figure 3.3 shows an example of another stack block. This block will repeatedly execute any code blocks that you choose to embed inside it for as long as a tested condition evaluates as true.

Note

You will learn about the application of repetitive and conditional programming logic in Chapter 9.

Figure 3.2
An example of a code block that is used to halt the playback of an audio file.

Figure 3.3
This code block allows other stack blocks to be embedded within it.

Some stack blocks include an input area inside them that allows you to specify a value by typing in a number. For example, the stack block shown in Figure 3.4 lets you assign the color to be used when drawing by inserting a color-associated numeric value.

To modify the value assigned to a block like the one shown in Figure 3.4, click on the white area within the code block and type in a new value. Some code blocks

 ———— Editable Text
                                              Field

Figure 3.4
This code block is used to specify the color to be used when drawing.

Figure 3.5
This code block has a pull-down menu that you can use to configure how it operates.

let you configure them by selecting a value from a pull-down list, as demonstrated in Figure 3.5.

Working with Hat Blocks

A *hat block* is a code block with a rounded or curved top and a bump at the bottom, visually indicating that it can be snapped on top of other stack blocks. Hat blocks provide the ability to create event-driven scripts. An *event-driven* script is one that automatically executes when a specified event occurs. An example of an event that can automatically trigger script execution is when the user clicks on the green flag button. When this event occurs, any scripts that begin with the hat block shown in Figure 3.6 are automatically executed.

Script execution can also be triggered when the user clicks on a sprite. This can be set up by adding the code block shown in Figure 3.7 to the beginning of the script.

Note

Every sprite in an application can potentially have its own scripts. You can automate the execution of any or all of the scripts using hat blocks. In addition to sprites, the stage can also have scripts.

Working with Reporter Blocks

A third type of Scratch code block is a reporter block. A *reporter block* is a code block that has either rounded or angled sides and is specifically designed as a mechanism for providing input for other code blocks to process. For example, the code block shown in Figure 3.8 is a typical reporter block.

Figure 3.6
This hat block automatically runs a script when the user clicks on the green flag.

Figure 3.7
This hat block runs a script whenever the user clicks on the sprite to which this script belongs.

Figure 3.8
This code block retrieves a numeric value indicating a sprite's volume.

Figure 3.9
You can provide input to this code block by either keying it in or using a reporter block.

Figure 3.10
Angled report blocks pass Boolean data to other code blocks for processing.

Figure 3.11
This code block pauses script execution until a specified event is true.

Figure 3.12
This particular combination of code blocks will pause script execution until the user presses the spacebar.

As you can see, this reporter block has rounded sides. As such, it can only fit into code blocks like the one shown in Figure 3.9, whose input area displays a shape with rounded sides.

Figure 3.10 shows an example of a reporter block that has angled sides. This particular code block returns a value of true if the user has pressed the spacebar or a false if the spacebar has not been pressed. Because it has angled sides, it can only be embedded inside code blocks that contain an input area whose sides are also angled.

Note

Boolean is a term used to represent data that has one of two values, either true or false.

To take advantage of a reporter block like the one shown in Figure 3.10, you need to embed the reporter block into another code block that has been designed to work with it. For example, Figure 3.11 shows one such code block.

Figure 3.12 demonstrates how a reporter blocks looks after being embedded within another code block.

Keeping an Eye Out with Monitors

You have probably noticed that Scratch displays a small check box just to the left of certain code blocks in the blocks palette, as demonstrated in Figure 3.13.

Figure 3.13
An example of a code block capable of displaying a monitor on the stage.

Figure 3.14
By default, a monitor displays the name of its associated code block.

Figure 3.15
Monitors can be configured to display a large readout.

Figure 3.16
Variable monitors also support a display format that includes a slider bar.

The presence of a check box indicates that the code block is capable of displaying a monitor on the stage. A *monitor* is a small block that displays the value currently assigned to the code block. To display the monitor, just click on the check box to select it. When you do so, a gray block is automatically displayed on the stage, as demonstrated in Figure 3.14.

You can modify the way the monitor looks by right-clicking on it and selecting Large Readout from the popup menu that appears. As a result, the appearance of the monitor will change, as demonstrated in Figure 3.15.

Tip

You can also toggle between monitor formats by double-clicking on the monitor.

Variable-based monitors support a third format, which includes a slider bar, as demonstrated in Figure 3.16. You will learn about variables and their use in Chapter 7, "Storing and Retrieving Data."

Eight Categories of Scratch Blocks

Scratch provides access to over 100 code blocks. These code blocks are organized into eight categories and are made available on the blocks palette. Each of these categories of code blocks is described in the following list:

- **Motion.** Code blocks that control sprite placement, direction, rotation, and movement.

- **Looks.** Code blocks that affect sprite and background appearance and provide the ability to display text.

- **Sound.** Code blocks that control the playback and volume of musical notes and audio files.

- **Pen.** Code blocks that can be used to draw using different colors and pen sizes.

- **Control.** Code blocks that trigger script execution based on predefined events, repeatedly execute programming logic using loops, and perform conditional logic.

- **Sensing.** Code blocks that can be used to determine the location of the mouse-pointer, its distance from other sprites, and whether a sprite is touching another sprite.

- **Numbers.** Code blocks that perform logical comparisons, rounding, and other arithmetic operations.

- **Variables.** Code blocks that can be used to store data used by applications when they execute.

You can view the code blocks belonging to a given category by clicking on one of the eight labeled button controls at the top of the blocks palette. Note that each category of code block is color coded, making it easy to distinguish between code blocks from different categories.

Each of these categories of code blocks is reviewed in the sections that follow. This review covers Scratch's entire collection of code blocks, indicating which ones support monitors and providing a brief description of each block's usage.

Moving Objects Around the Drawing Canvas

Motion blocks control a sprite's placement on the stage. Motion blocks are colored blue. There are motion blocks that let you set the direction a sprite will move and then other blocks to move them. There are also motions blocks that report on a sprite's location and direction. Table 3.1 outlines all of the code blocks that fit into this category.

Table 3.1   Scratch Motion Blocks

Block	Monitor	Description
move 10 steps	No	Moves a sprite forward or backwards a specified number of steps.
turn ↻ 15 degrees	No	Rotates a sprite a specified number of degrees in a clockwise direction.
turn ↺ 15 degrees	No	Rotates a sprite a specified number of degrees in a counterclockwise direction.
point in direction 90 ▾	No	Points a sprite toward a specified direction (0 = up, 90 = right, −90 = left, 180 = down).
point towards ▾	No	Points a sprite toward either the mouse-pointer or a specified sprite.
go to x: 0 y: 0	No	Moves a sprite to a specified coordination location on the stage.
go to ▾	No	Moves a sprite to the location of either the mouse-pointer or another sprite.
glide 1 secs to x: 0 y: 0	No	Moves a sprite to the specified coordinate position over a specified number of seconds.
change x by 10	No	Changes the position of a sprite on the X-axis by a specified number of pixels.
set x to 0	No	Changes a sprite's location on the X-axis to a specified value.
change y by 10	No	Changes the position of a sprite on the Y-axis by a specified number of pixels.
set y to 0	No	Changes a sprite's location on the Y-axis to a specified value.
if on edge, bounce	No	Changes a sprite's direction when it makes contact with one of the edges of the stage.
x position	Yes	Retrieves a value representing a sprite's coordinate on the X-axis (between −240 and 240).
y position	Yes	Retrieves a value representing a sprite's coordinate on the Y-axis (between −180 and 180).
direction	Yes	Retrieves a value representing a sprite's current direction (0 = up, 90 = right, −90 = left, 180 = down).

You will learn more about motion blocks in Chapter 5, "Moving Things Around."

Changing Object Appearance

Looks blocks modify sprite and background appearance and display text within popup bubbles. Looks blocks are colored purple. There are looks blocks that let

Table 3.2 Scratch Looks Blocks

Block	Monitor	Description
switch to costume costume2	No	Changes a sprite's costume, modifying its appearance.
next costume	No	Changes a sprite's costume to the next costume in the sprite's costume list, jumping back to the beginning of the list when the end of the list is reached.
costume #	Yes	Retrieves a numeric value representing a sprite's current costume number.
say Hello! for 2 secs	No	Displays a text message in a speech bubble for a specified number of seconds.
say Hello!	No	Displays a text message in a speech bubble or removes the display of a speech bubble when no text is specified.
think Hmm... for 2 secs	No	Displays a text message in a thought bubble for a specified number of seconds.
think Hmm...	No	Displays a text message in a thought bubble or removes the display of a thought bubble when no text is specified.
change color effect by 25	No	Modifies a sprite's appearance by applying and modifying a special effect (color, fisheye, whirl, pixelate, mosaic, brightness, or ghost) by a specified numeric value.
set color effect to 0	No	Applies a special effect (color, fisheye, whirl, pixelate, mosaic, brightness, or ghost) to a sprite by a specified numeric value.
clear graphic effects	No	Restores a sprite to its normal appearance, removing any special effects that may have been applied.

Table 3.2 (Continued)

Block	Monitor	Description
change size by 10	No	Modifies the size of a sprite by a specified numeric amount.
set size to 100 %	No	Sets a sprite's size to a percentage of its original size.
size	Yes	Retrieves a percentage value representing a sprite's current size when compared to its original size.
show	No	Tells Scratch to display a sprite.
hide	No	Suppresses the display of a sprite on the stage, preventing it from interacting with other sprites.
go to front	No	Places a sprite on top of other sprites, placing it on the top layer and ensuring its display.
go back 1 layers	No	Moves a sprite back a specified number of layers, allowing other sprites to be displayed on top of it.
switch to background background1	No	Alters the stage's appearance by assigning it a different background.
next background	No	Changes the stage's background to the next background in the background list.
background #	No	Retrieves a numeric value representing the background number of the stage's current background.

you modify sprite costumes and colors. There are also blocks that let you modify a sprite's size and control whether a sprite is visible on the stage. Table 3.2 outlines all of the code blocks that fit into this category.

You will learn more about looks blocks in Chapter 10, "Changing the Way Sprites Look and Behave."

Making Some Noise

Sound blocks play music and add sound effects to your Scratch application projects. Sound blocks are colored pink. There are sound blocks that let you play sounds and drum beats, select different types of instruments, control playback volume, and modify tempo. Table 3.3 outlines all of the code blocks that fit into this category.

Table 3.3 Scratch Sound Blocks

Block	Monitor	Description
play sound meow	No	Plays the specified sound file while allowing the script file in which it is inserted to keep executing.
play sound meow until done	No	Plays the specified sound file, pausing script execution until the sound file has finished playing.
stop all sounds	No	Halts the playback of any sound files currently being played.
play drum 48 for 0.2 beats	No	Plays a drum sound selected from the block's pull-down menu a specified number of seconds.
rest for 0.2 beats	No	Pauses sound playback for a specified number of beats.
play note 60 for 0.5 beats	No	Plays a musical note selected from the block's pull-down menu a specified number of beats.
set instrument to 1	No	Specifies the instrument to be used when playing musical notes.
change volume by -10	No	Changes a sprite's volume by a specified value.
set volume to 100 %	No	Sets a sprite's sound volume to a specified percentage level.
volume	Yes	Retrieves a numeric value representing a sprite's sound volume.
change tempo by 20	No	Alters a sprite's tempo by a specified number of beats per minute.
set tempo to 60 bpm	No	Assigns the number of beats per minute to be used as a sprite's tempo.
tempo	Yes	Retrieves a numeric value representing a sprite's tempo.

You will learn more about sound blocks in Chapter 11, "Spicing Things Up with Sounds."

Drawing Lines and Shapes

Pen blocks draw any combination of shapes and lines using a virtual pen. Pen blocks are colored mint green. There are pen blocks that let you enable and disable drawing, set color and pen size, and apply shading. Table 3.4 outlines all of the code blocks that fit into this category.

You will learn more about pen blocks in Chapter 12, "Drawing Lines and Shapes."

Table 3.4 Scratch Pen Blocks

Block	Monitor	Description
clear	No	Erases or clears away anything drawn by the pen or stamped from the stage.
pen down	No	Places the pen in a down position, allowing drawing operations to occur as the pen is moved around the stage.
pen up	No	Disables drawing operations by lifting the pen.
set pen color to ■	No	Specifies the color to be used when drawing.
change pen color by 10	No	Changes the color used when drawing by a specified amount.
set pen color to 0	No	Specifies the color to be used when drawing based on a numeric range in which 0 is red (at the low end of the spectrum) and 100 equals blue (at the high end of the spectrum).
change pen shade by 10	No	Modifies the shading used when drawing by a specified amount.
set pen shade to 50	No	Specifies the shade to be used when drawing based on a numeric range in which 0 is the darkest possible shading and 100 represents the maximum possible amount of light.
change pen size by 1	No	Modifies the thickness of the pen based on a numeric increment.
set pen size to 1	No	Specifies the thickness or width of the pen used when drawing.
stamp	No	Draws or stamps the image of a sprite onto the stage.

Looping, Conditional Logic, and Event Programming

Control blocks automate the execution of scripts, pause script execution, and send messages to other sprites, allowing sprites to synchronize their execution. There are also control blocks that let you set up loops to repeatedly execute collections of code blocks as well as control blocks that let you conditionally execute other code blocks based on whether or not a test condition evaluates as true. Control blocks are colored gold. Table 3.5 outlines all of the code blocks that fit into this category.

You will learn more about control blocks in Chapter 9.

Sensing Sprite Location and Environmental Input

Sensing blocks determine the location of the mouse-pointer, its distance from other sprites, and whether a sprite is touching another sprite. Sensing blocks are

Table 3.5 Scratch Control Blocks

Block	Monitor	Description
when 🏁 clicked	No	Executes the script to which it has been attached whenever the IDE's green flag button is pressed.
when space key pressed	No	Executes the script to which it has been attached whenever a specified keyboard key is pressed.
when Sprite1 clicked	No	Executes the script to which it has been attached whenever the user clicks on the sprite to which the script belongs.
wait 1 secs	No	Pauses script execution for a specified number of seconds, after which the script resumes its execution.
forever	No	Repeatedly executes all of the code blocks embedded inside it.
repeat 10	No	Repeats the execution of all the code blocks embedded inside it a specified number of times.
broadcast ▼	No	Specifies a broadcast message to all sprites without pausing script execution.
broadcast ▼ and wait	No	Sends a broadcast message to all sprites to trigger a predefined action and then pauses script execution, waiting until all sprites have completed their assigned action before allowing the script in which the block resides to continue executing.
when I receive ▼	No	Executes the scripts to which it has been attached when a specified broadcast message is received.
forever if ◯	No	Repeatedly executes all of the code blocks embedded within the control for as long as the specified condition evaluates as true.
if ◯	No	Executes all of the code blocks embedded within the control if the specified condition evaluates as true.
if ◯ else	No	Executes all of the code blocks embedded in the top half of the control (between the If an Else) if the specified condition evaluates as true and executes all of the code blocks embedded in the bottom half of the control (after Else) if the condition evaluates as being false.
wait until ◯	No	Pauses script execution until a specified condition becomes true.
repeat until ◯	No	Repeats all of the code blocks embedded inside it for as long as a tested condition evaluates as true.

Table 3.5 (Continued)

Block	Monitor	Description
stop script	No	Halts a script's execution.
stop all	No	Halts the execution of all scripts for all sprites in the application.

colored sky blue. There are sensing blocks that can be used to interact with Scratch boards, allowing applications to detect when the sensor board's buttons or slider are being pressed. Table 3.6 outlines all of the code blocks that fit into this category.

Note

A *Scratch board* is a special piece of hardware that you can purchase from the Scratch website and attach to your computer. Once it is attached, you can use a sensor board to collect and process environment- and user-provided input. You will learn how to programmatically interact with and control Scratch boards in Chapter 14, "Collecting External Input Using a Scratch Sensor Board."

You will learn more about sensing blocks in Chapter 6, "Sensing Sprite Position and Controlling Environmental Settings."

Working with Numbers

Numbers blocks perform arithmetic operations, generate random numbers, and compare numeric values to determine their relationship to one another. Numbers blocks are green. There are numbers blocks that can be used to round numeric values and to execute a host of mathematical functions like determining absolute value or square root of a number. Table 3.7 outlines all of the code blocks that fit into this category.

You will learn more about number blocks in Chapter 8, "Doing a Little Math."

Storing and Retrieving Data

Variables blocks store and retrieve numeric values in computer memory. You will need to use variables to store data as your application executes. For example, if you create a game that challenges the player to try and guess a randomly

Table 3.6 Scratch Sensing Blocks

Block	Monitor	Description
mouse x	No	Retrieves the location of the mouse-pointer on the X-axis.
mouse y	No	Retrieves the location of the mouse-pointer on the Y-axis.
mouse down?	No	Retrieves a Boolean value of true or false, depending on whether a mouse button is pressed.
key space pressed?	No	Retrieves a Boolean value of true or false, depending on whether a specified key is pressed.
touching ?	No	Retrieves a Boolean value of true or false, depending on whether the sprite is touching a specified sprite, edge, or mouse-pointer as selected from the block's pull-down menu.
touching color ?	No	Retrieves a Boolean value of true of false, depending on whether the sprite is touching a specified color.
color is touching ?	No	Retrieves a Boolean value of true of false, depending on whether the first specified color inside the sprite is touching the second specified color on the background or on another sprite.
distance to	No	Retrieves a numeric value representing a sprite's distance from another sprite or from the mouse-pointer.
reset timer	No	Resets the timer back to its default value of zero.
timer	Yes	Retrieves a numeric value representing the number of seconds that the timer has run.
x position of Sprite1	No	Retrieves the property value (x position, y position, direction, customer #, and size of volume) for the background of a specified sprite.
loudness	Yes	Retrieves a numeric value, from 1 to 100, representing the volume of the computer's microphone.
loud?	Yes	Retrieves a Boolean value of true or false when a sound value of 30 or greater is detected through the computer's microphone.
slider sensor value	Yes	Retrieves the value being reported by one of the sensors on a Scratch board.
sensor button pressed ?	Yes	Retrieves a Boolean value of true or false, depending on whether a specified sensor is being pressed.

generated number, you will need to use a variable to store and refer back to this number.

Variables can be used in conjunction with conditional programming logic to control the execution of other code blocks. Variables can also be used to control

Table 3.7 Scratch Numbers Blocks

Block	Monitor	Description
+	No	Adds two numbers together and generates a result.
-	No	Subtracts one number from another and returns the result.
*	No	Multiplies two numbers together and generates a result.
/	No	Divides one number into another and returns the result.
pick random 1 to 10	No	Generates a random number within the specified range.
<	No	Returns a Boolean value of true or false, depending on whether one number is less than another.
=	No	Returns a Boolean value of true or false, depending on whether one number is equal to another.
>	No	Returns a Boolean value of true or false, depending on whether one number is greater than another.
and	No	Returns a Boolean value of true or false, depending on whether two separately evaluated conditions are both true.
or	No	Returns a Boolean value of true or false, depending on whether either of two separately evaluated conditions is true.
not	No	Reverses the Boolean value from true to false or false to true.
mod	No	Retrieves the remainder portion of a division operation between two numbers.
round	No	Returns the nearest integer value for a specified number.
sqrt of 10	No	Returns the result of the selected function (abs, sqrt, sin, cos, tan, asin, acos, atan, Ln, log, E^, and 10^) when applied to the specified number.

the repeated execution of code blocks embedded within code block loops. Variables blocks are colored orange. You can create and name custom variables blocks and assign them a starting value. You can also modify their values during script execution. Other code blocks can retrieve variable values and use them as input. Table 3.8 outlines all of the code blocks that fit into this category.

You will learn more about variables blocks in Chapter 7.

Table 3.8 Scratch Variables Blocks

Block	Monitor	Description
change PlayerScore by 1	No	Modifies the value assigned to a numeric value stored in a variable by the specified amount.
set PlayerScore to 0	No	Assigns a value to a numeric variable.
PlayerScore	Yes	Retrieves the value assigned to a variable.

Getting Help with Code Blocks

In addition to bookmarking and referring back to the tables provided in this chapter to find out what a given code block does, you can view help information for any Scratch code block by right-clicking on the code block in the blocks palette, as demonstrated in Figure 3.17.

Alternatively, you can right-click on a code block once it has been added to the scripts area to access a link to the block's help file, as demonstrated in Figure 3.18.

By clicking on the Help link in the popup menu that is displayed, you can display help information for that control. For example, Figure 3.19 shows the help information that is available for the forever code block.

As Figure 3.19 shows, the help information that is displayed explains the purpose of the code block and demonstrates its usage.

Figure 3.17
Accessing help for a given Scratch code block.

Figure 3.18
Accessing help for a Scratch code block that has been added to the scripts area.

Figure 3.19
Displaying the help window for the `forever` code block.

Summary

This chapter provided a quick reference that outlined the purpose and usage of all of the code blocks provided by Scratch. You may want to bookmark this chapter to help make it easy to return to and take advantage of this information. This chapter explained the three types of code blocks supported by Scratch and outlined their relationship to one another. The chapter then provided an explanation of all 100 plus Scratch code blocks, going over them category by category. On top of all this, you learned how to work with and configure monitors and to access help information for individual code blocks.

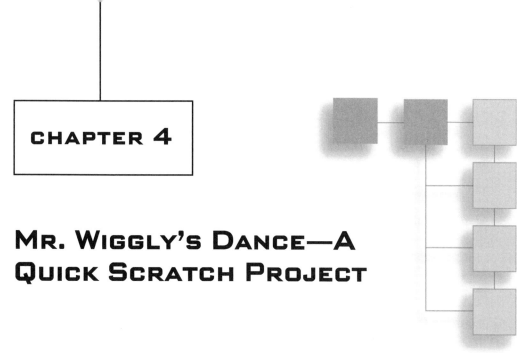

CHAPTER 4

MR. WIGGLY'S DANCE—A QUICK SCRATCH PROJECT

So far, you have been presented with an overview of Scratch and its capabilities and learned how to work with its IDE. You have also been given an overview of all of the code blocks that make up the Scratch programming language and learned the basic steps involved in creating Scratch applications. Now that you are more familiar with Scratch and its key components, let's put this new knowledge to use by creating a new Scratch application project, examining in greater detail the steps involved in creating and executing Scratch applications.

The topics covered in this chapter include:

- A review of the programming concepts that Scratch can teach you

- A detailed overview of how to build Scratch applications

- Learning how to distribute your Scratch programs on CD-ROM

Programming with Scratch

As a beginner's programming language, Scratch teaches you a number of critical programming concepts that you will be able to later rely on should you decide to make the jump to other more traditional and industrial-strength programming languages like Microsoft Visual Basic, C++, JavaScript, and

AppleScript. The programming concepts that you can learn from Scratch include:

- **Sequential Processing.** This involves the processing of application code blocks, in the order that they are laid out, starting at the beginning of a script file and continuing to the end of the script.

- **Conditional Programming Logic.** This involves the conditional execution of code blocks based on data collected during application execution.

- **Use of Variables.** This involves the storage, retrieval, and modification of data during application execution.

- **Iterative Processing.** This involves the repeated execution of code blocks to process large amounts of information or to control the repeated execution of code blocks required to direct the execution of a game or application.

- **Boolean Logic.** This involves the application of programming logic that executes based on the analysis of true/false data provided by Scratch during program execution.

- **Interface Design.** This involves the development of user-friendly and intuitive application stage layout, making it easy for users to interact with applications.

- **Program Synchronization.** This involves the passage and receipt of messages between application scripts for the purpose of coordinating the execution of different parts of an application.

- **Event Handling.** This involves the initiation of script execution based on the occurrence of predefined events, such as the pressing of keyboard keys, the pressing of the green flag key, or the receipt of a synchronization message.

- **Application and Game Development.** This involves the creation of different types of computer application projects.

- **Sprite Programming.** This involves the use of sprites as the basis for developing graphical programs.

- **Application Troubleshooting.** This involves the identification, location, and elimination of programming errors, or bugs, that prevent applications from executing as they are supposed to.

You will learn more about each of these programming concepts as you make your way through the remainder of this book.

Note

As powerful and fun as Scratch is, there are some programming concepts that it does not teach. These concepts include the storage of collections of data in arrays, the ability to process file input and output, the ability to organize application code into procedures, and the ability to support advanced object-oriented programming techniques. However, as a first-time programmer, these concepts can be challenging to learn, and by omitting them, the developers of Scratch have produced a streamlined yet powerful learning environment, which will prepare you to later make the jump to programming languages that support these advanced programming concepts.

Creating the Mr. Wiggly's Dance Application

The rest of this chapter is dedicated to leading you through the development of the Mr. Wiggly's Dance application. In this Scratch application, a short, round, and comical cartoonish character named Mr. Wiggly dances around the stage to music, as demonstrated in Figure 4.1.

Because Mr. Wiggly is bashful, his skin changes color as he dances, as demonstrated in Figure 4.2. Although not immediately obvious when viewed in black and white, if you compare the color of Mr. Wiggly in Figures 4.1 and 4.2, you will notice that he has definitely begun to blush, betraying his discomfort at dancing in front of an audience.

Figure 4.1
Mr. Wiggly practices his dance moves, dancing back and forth across the stage.

Figure 4.2
The bashful Mr. Wiggly's skin color changes as he dances.

Figure 4.3
Mr. Wiggly pauses at the end of each dance only to decide to keep dancing.

At the end of each dance, Mr. Wiggly pauses for a moment to reflect on how things are going before deciding to keep on dancing, as demonstrated in Figure 4.3.

The Mr. Wiggly's Dance application project will be created by following a series of steps, as outlined here:

1. Creating a new Scratch application project.

2. Adding a project background.

3. Adding and removing sprites to and from the project.

4. Importing a music file into the application.

5. Scripting audio playback.

6. Adding the programming logic required to make Mr. Wiggly dance.

7. Saving and executing your work.

Since this book has yet to provide a detailed explanation of how to work with all of the Scratch code blocks used in this application project, brief explanations will be provided. You will learn the ins and out of programming with code blocks in Chapters 5 through 12. As you make your way through each of the steps in this project, try and keep your focus on the overall process being followed and do not get caught up in the specifics. Later, once you have finished reviewing Chapters 5 through 12, you can always return and review this project again and clear up any questions you may have.

Step 1: Creating a New Scratch Project

The first step in creating a Scratch project is to start Scratch. Doing so results in the automatic creation of a new Scratch project. New Scratch projects come equipped with a single sprite with two costumes representing a cat. You can choose to incorporate this sprite into your application or to remove it. If, on the other hand, Scratch has already been started and you have been working with it for a while, you can create and open a new Scratch application project by clicking on the New button located on the Scratch menu bar. In response, a new project is opened in the IDE, as shown in Figure 4.4.

Step 2: Adding a Background to the Stage

With your new Scratch application project now created, it is time to get to work. Let's begin by adding a suitable background to the stage that will help set the mood of the application. Backgrounds are associated with the stage, so to add a background to your application, you must click on the blank stage thumbnail located in the sprite list. Once selected, the stage thumbnail is highlighted with a blue outline, as shown in Figure 4.5.

Once you have selected the stage thumbnail, you can modify its background by clicking on the Backgrounds tab located at the top of the scripts area. When you do so, the currently assigned stage background is displayed, as shown in Figure 4.6.

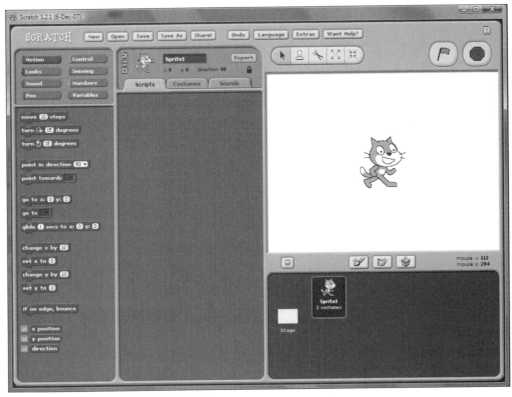

Figure 4.4
New Scratch application projects come supplied with a single sprite.

Figure 4.5
Selected thumbnails in the sprite list are highlighted with a blue outline.

To replace the currently assigned blank background with something more interesting, click on the Import button. This will open the Import Background window. Once opened, click on the Indoors folder, select the chalkboard thumbnail, as shown in Figure 4.7, and click on the OK button.

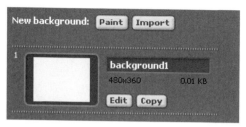

Figure 4.6
The Backgrounds tab provides the ability to create, import, edit, and rename backgrounds.

Figure 4.7
Importing a new background into your Scratch application project.

Once imported, the new background will be added to the application's current list of background files, as shown in Figure 4.8. As you can see, the thumbnail is automatically assigned a name and a number.

Since this application only requires one background, you can remove the default blank background named background1 from your project by clicking on the Delete This Costume button, which is located to the right of the background's picture and represented by a round X button.

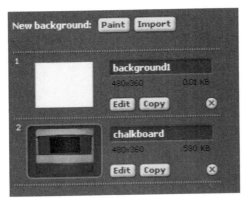

Figure 4.8
Scratch applications can have any number of backgrounds and can switch between them during execution.

Figure 4.9
Click on the Choose New Sprite from File button to access a collection of ready-made sprites.

Tip

Removing backgrounds, costumes, and sound files no longer needed by your Scratch applications will reduce their size. This can be of critical importance should you decide to upload them to the Scratch website. There is a 10MB project size limit at that site. Graphic and audio files tend to be relatively large, so removing any that you do not need can have a significant impact on the size of your applications.

Step 3: Adding and Removing Sprites

The next step in the development of this Scratch project is to add a sprite representing Mr. Wiggly to the project and to remove the cat sprite, which is not needed in this application. To add the sprite representing Mr. Wiggly, click on the Choose New Sprite from File button, as shown in Figure 4.9. This button is the middle button that makes up the collection of new sprite buttons, located just beneath the stage and just above the sprite list.

Scratch provides ready access to all kinds of sprites, organized into the following six folders:

- Animals

- Fantasy

- Letters

- People

- Things

- Transportation

The sprite that you want to use to represent Mr. Wiggly is located in the People folder. Once clicked, the Choose New Sprite from File button instructs Scratch to display the New Sprite window, which provides access to the six folders listed above. Open the People folder and then scroll down until you locate the roundman sprite, as shown in Figure 4.10.

Select the roundman sprite by clicking on it and then click on the OK button. The New Sprite window will close and the new sprite will be added to the middle of the stage, as shown in Figure 4.11.

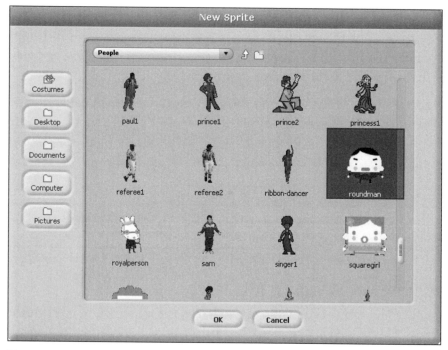

Figure 4.10
Selecting the sprite that will be used to represent Mr Wiggly.

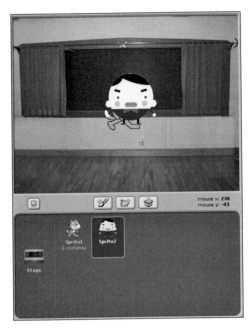

Figure 4.11
A thumbnail representing the sprite is also added to the sprite list.

When contrasted against the stage's background, Mr. Wiggly's default placement in the middle of the stage makes it look like he is floating on air. To put things into proper perspective, drag and drop Mr. Wiggly about one inch lower down the stage, so that it looks like he is standing on the floor.

Since the Mr. Wiggly's Dance application does not need the default cat sprite, go ahead and remove this sprite from the application project by selecting the Delete button on the Scratch toolbar and then clicking on the thumbnail for the cat located in the sprite list.

Tip

You can also remove the cat sprite from the application by right-clicking on its thumbnail and then selecting Delete from the popup menu that is displayed.

Step 4: Adding Mr. Wiggly's Music

Now that you have taken care of the sprites needed by the application, it is time to import the sound file. To do this, click on the thumbnail representing the stage in the sprite list and then click on the Sounds tab in the scripts area. In response, Scratch will display all of the sound files belonging to the sprite. By default, every

Figure 4.12
All sprites supplied by Scratch come equipped with the same sound file.

sprite in a Scratch application is assigned a common sound file named pop, as shown in Figure 4.12.

Scratch provides ready access to all kinds of prerecorded audio files. The name of the sound file that Mr. Wiggly will dance to is Eggs. To add this file to the sprite, click on the Import button. In response, Scratch will display the Import Sound window, which by default contains eight folders, listed next, in which Scratch stores its audio files.

- Animal

- Effects

- Electronic

- Human

- Instruments

- Music Loops

- Percussion

- Vocals

Drill down into the Music Loops folder by double-clicking on it. Locate and click on the Eggs file, as shown in Figure 4.13. Scratch will immediately play the file, so you can hear what it sounds like.

Click on the OK button to import the sound file into your application project, as demonstrated in Figure 4.14. Note that for each sound file, a number of pieces of information are displayed. You can see the name of the file, the length of time that it takes to play the file, and the file's size. Note that the Eggs sound file takes

Figure 4.13
Importing a sound file into a Scratch application project.

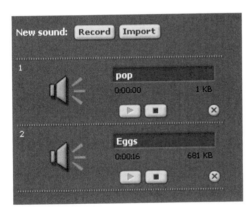

Figure 4.14
You can add any number of sound files to a sprite.

16 second to play. You will need to remember this information a little later when programming the playback of this sound file.

The default pop sound file is not needed by this application; therefore, you can delete it by clicking on the round Delete This Sound button located at the bottom-right side of the sound file entry.

Step 5: Playing the Dance Music

It is time to begin putting together the program code logic required to make your new application work. In total you will need to create two scripts for this project: one for the stage and another for the sprite representing Mr. Wiggly. The script belonging to the stage will be made up of code blocks that are responsible for playing the application's background music. The script belonging to the sprite will contain the programming logic required to make Mr. Wiggly dance.

The first step in the development of the stage's script is to click on the Control button in the blocks palette and then to drag and drop an instance of the when green flag clicked block onto the scripts area, as demonstrated in Figure 4.15. This hat code block will automatically execute the script to which it is attached whenever the green flag button is clicked.

Since the application's background music is supposed to be played over and over again for as long as the application runs, you need to set up a loop that will repeatedly play the sound file. To set this up, drag and drop an instance of the forever code block to the scripts area, attaching it to the bottom of the when green flag clicked block, as shown in Figure 4.16.

Now that you have the loop set up, click on the Sound button located at the top of the blocks palette and then drag and drop an instance of the play sound code block onto the scripts area, embedding it inside the forever code block. Next, click on the pull-down menu located on the right-hand side of the code block and select Eggs from the list that appears. At this point the script that you are developing should look like the example shown in Figure 4.17.

Note

Scratch automatically populates the play sound code block with a list of all of the sound files that you added previously to the stage, making it easy for you to access them when working with sound code blocks.

At this point you only need to add one last code block to the script to finish it up. To do so, click on the Control button located at the top of the blocks palette and then drag and drop an instance of the wait secs code block over the scripts area, inserting it inside the forever code block, immediately following the play sound block, as shown in Figure 4.18. This block is needed to pause the loop for 16 seconds, allowing for the complete playback of the sound file, before the loop repeats and begins playing it again.

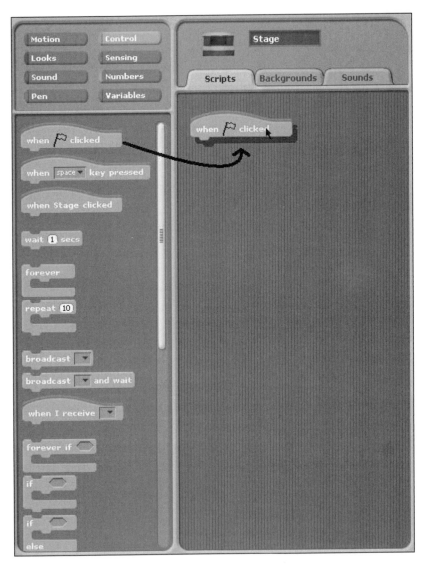

Figure 4.15
This block will be used to automatically execute the script whenever the green flag button is clicked.

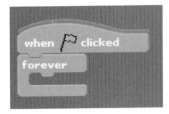

Figure 4.16
The forever block will repeat the execution of any code block that you embed within it.

Figure 4.17
Using the play sound code block to play back the Eggs sound file.

Figure 4.18
Pausing loop execution to allow playback of the sound file to complete.

Note

Now that this script has been written, you can test it out by double-clicking on it. In response, Scratch will repeatedly play back the sound file. Once you are convinced that everything is working correctly, click on the red Stop Everything button to halt the script's execution so that you can move on to the next step in the development of this application.

Note

In addition to playing an audio file using the combination of the sound and control blocks shown in Figure 4.18, you can instead use the code block shown here, which does the same thing as these two code blocks.

Step 6: Making Mr. Wiggly Dance

Now that you have finished work on the stage's script, it is time to write the script that makes Mr. Wiggly dance. To do so, click on the thumbnail of the sprite representing Mr. Wiggly (in the sprite area). In response, Scratch should clear out the script's area and automatically select the Scripts tab for you so that you can begin script development.

The first step in the development of this is to click on the Control button in the blocks palette and then to drag and drop an instance of the when green flag clicked block onto the scripts area, as demonstrated in Figure 4.19. This hat code block will automatically execute the script to which it is attached whenever the green flag button is clicked.

In this application, Mr. Wiggly is supposed to dance over and over again without stopping (until the user stops running the application). To set this up, drag and drop an instance of the forever code block onto the scripts area and attach it to the bottom of the when green flag clicked block, as shown in Figure 4.20.

Next, it is time to add a pair of code statements that will move Mr. Wiggly 25 steps to the right and then pause for two seconds. This is accomplished by dragging and dropping the move steps and wait secs blocks to the scripts area, embedding them inside the forever code block, as shown in Figure 4.21. Note

Figure 4.19
Setting up the script to execute when the green flag is clicked.

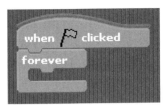

Figure 4.20
Adding a loop to the script to repeat the execution of embedded code blocks.

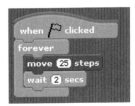

Figure 4.21
Adding the programming logic that makes Mr. Wiggly dance his first step.

Figure 4.22
Adding the remaining code blocks required to complete Mr. Wiggly's dance routine.

that by default the move steps block is set to 10. You will need to replace this with a value of 25.

Next, you need to add a series of move steps and wait secs code blocks, which, when executed, will move Mr. Wiggly 25 steps to the right followed by four moves to the left at 25 steps each and then another two moves back towards the right. This is accomplished by adding seven sets of a code block, as shown in Figure 4.22.

To complete the development of this script, you need to add two looks blocks, as shown in Figure 4.23. The change effect by code block is used to modify Mr. Wiggly's color each time the loop finishes its execution, simulating the feeling of embarrassment that Mr. Wiggly experiences when he dances. Lastly, the think for secs code block is used to display a text message in a popup bubble that shows Mr. Wiggly thinking about and then deciding to keep dancing.

Figure 4.23
Modifying Mr. Wiggly's color and displaying his thoughts.

Step 7: Saving and Executing Your New Scratch Application

At this point your copy of the Mr. Wiggly's Dance application should be complete. All that remains is for you to save the application and then to execute it and see how it looks when running. To save your application, click on the Save button located on the IDE's menu bar. In response, Scratch will display the Save Project window, as demonstrated in Figure 4.24, prompting you to specify the name and location where you want to store your new application.

In addition, Scratch provides the opportunity to enter your name as the project author and to enter notes describing the project in the Project Author and About This Project text fields. Once you are done, click on the OK button to save your Scratch application project.

Once you have saved your work, run the application to see how it works. Since both of the application's scripts are configured to execute whenever the green flag button is pressed, all you have to do is click on that button and sit back and watch as the bashful Mr. Wiggly dances about the stage for your amusement.

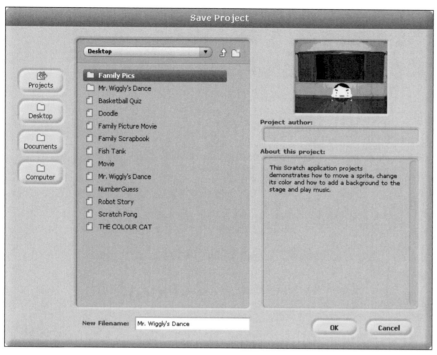

Figure 4.24
Saving your copy of the Mr. Wiggly's Dance application project.

Distributing Scratch Projects

Scratch is an interpreted programming language. This means that unlike some programming languages, such as Visual Basic and C++, which compile their applications into an executable file that can then be run on other computers without requiring that the programming language be installed, Scratch applications can only execute when run within the Scratch IDE (or on the Scratch website at http://scratch.mit.edu). Therefore, if you want to distribute your Scratch applications and have them execute on someone else's computer, you must first see to it that Scratch is installed on the other computer, or you must create a special application distribution CD that includes Scratch system files required to run your application when Scratch has not been installed.

Note

You can also share access to your Scratch application projects by posting them on the Scratch website and pointing your friends to that website, where they can view and run them using a Java-enabled web browser. You will learn all about the steps involved in sharing your Scratch applications this way in Chapter 13, "Sharing Your Scratch Projects Over the Internet."

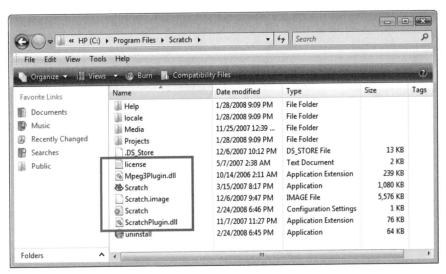

Figure 4.25
Burn a copy of the files shown in this figure along with your Scratch application file to create a distributable Windows CD-ROM.

Distributing Scratch Applications to Windows Computers

The files that you need to burn to your distribution CD-ROM vary, depending on whether you are working with Microsoft Windows or Mac OS X. When working with Microsoft Windows, you will need to burn the following files identified in Figure 4.25, as well as a copy of your Scratch application, to a CD-ROM.

Each of the files listed can be found in the folder in which you installed Scratch, which on Microsoft Windows is C:\Program Files\Scratch by default.

- Scratch.exe

- Scratch.image

- Scratch.ini

- ScratchPlugin.dll

- Mpeg3Plugin.dll

- License.txt

Note

The reason for including the License.txt file, which is Scratch's license document, is to ensure that anyone you distribute your CD-ROM to will know the terms of the license agreement. Including this file will also keep you out of legal trouble.

Distributing Scratch Applications to Mac OS X Computers

If you are working with Mac OS X and want to create a distribution disc to share your creations with other Mac users who do not have Scratch installed on their computers, you may do so by burning a CD-ROM containing your Scratch application projects as well as the following Scratch system files, all of which are available in Scratch's installation folder.

- Scratch.app

- Scratch.image

- License.txt

Instructions for Executing Your Application from a CD-ROM

Once you have burned a CD-ROM for your Scratch application, you need to tell your friends how to execute it, which can be done by double-clicking on Screatch.exe (Windows) or Scratch.app (Mac OS X), which will start the Scratch IDE, after which your application can be accessed by clicking on the IDE's Open button.

Alternatively, for Windows users, you might want to consider adding a batch file for each application that you added to the CD-ROM that when executed will run one of your Scratch applications. You can do this by opening your preferred text editor (such as Notepad) and keying in a single statement using the following syntax.

```
Scratch.exe Scratch.image ScratchProject.sb
```

Here, Scratch.exe is the name of the Scratch executable that starts Scratch. Scratch.image is a required Scratch system file, and *ScratchProject.sb* represents the name of a Scratch application that you have added to the CD-ROM. Note that the .sb file extension has been included. Once you have typed in this statement, save the text file with a filename that ends with a .bat file extension (MrWiggly.bat, HelloWorld.bat, etc.).

When a batch file is added to the CD-ROM along with all of the files already listed, your friends can start your Scratch application by double-clicking on it. Once double-clicked, the batch file will open Scratch and load your Scratch application project into it, making it ready for execution.

Summary

This chapter walked you through the development of your second Scratch project. In learning how to create Mr. Wiggly's Dance, you learned the fundamental steps involved in creating and executing Scratch applications. This included learning how to change stage backgrounds and work with sprites. Although detailed instruction on how to work with different code blocks and sounds is not covered until later chapters, you received a quick overview of how to work with a number of control, motion, looks, and sound blocks, and you learned how to import audio files and sprites into your Scratch applications.

PART II

LEARNING HOW TO WRITE
SCRATCH PROGRAMS

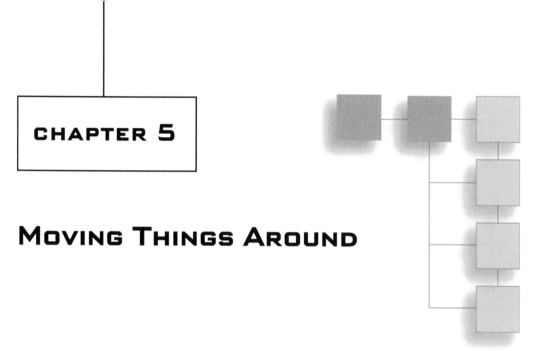

CHAPTER 5

MOVING THINGS AROUND

This chapter is the first of eight chapters designed to teach you how to work with all of the code blocks that make up the Scratch programming language. This chapter's focus is on demonstrating how to work with motion code blocks. Using these blocks, you will be able to create Scratch applications that can move sprites around the stage, rotate sprites, point them in different directions, change sprite location, detect collisions with the edge of the stage, and report on a sprite's direction and coordinates. This chapter also introduces you to Scratch cards as a means for learning how to perform different types of tasks. You will also learn how to create a new virtual fish tank application.

The major topics covered in this chapter include:

- Learning how to move and rotate sprites

- Learning how to change sprite direction and location

- Learning how to change sprite location and to detect collisions with the edge of the stage

- Learning how to retrieve and report information about a sprite's coordinates and direction

Working with Motion Code Blocks

To move sprites around the stage when your Scratch applications execute, you need to learn how to work with motion code blocks. As previously stated, motion blocks control sprite placement, direction, rotation, and movement. In total, Scratch provides access to 16 different motion blocks, which you can work with by clicking on the Motion button located at the top of the blocks palette and then dragging and dropping motion blocks onto the scripts area, where you can configure them and use them in creating scripts.

If you look closely at the various motion code blocks, you will notice that Scratch organizes them into six subgroupings, each of which is separated by a blank space in the blocks palette. These sub groupings include:

- Motion blocks that move and rotate sprites

- Motion blocks that point sprites in different directions or towards different objects

- Motion blocks that change a sprite's location and control whether a sprite jumps to its new location or glides to it

- Motion blocks that change a sprite location by setting or modifying the value of its X-axis and Y-axis coordinates

- A motion block that controls a sprite's movement when it touches the edges of the stage

- Motion blocks that report on a sprite's position and direction

Examples of how to work with the motion code blocks in each of these subgroups are provided throughout the rest of this chapter.

Moving and Rotating Sprites

Scratch provides access to three motion blocks that move sprites and rotate them on their axis. These code blocks are shown in Figure 5.1.

The first of these blocks allows you to specify the number of steps that a sprite should be moved on the stage (in whatever direction the sprite is currently pointing). By default, the code block specifies a value of 10. However, you may

Figure 5.1
These control blocks are designed to give you control over the relative movement and rotation of sprites.

change this value to suit your needs. You can even enter a negative value to move the sprite in the opposite direction that it is pointing.

In addition, you can drag and drop any reporter block you want into this code block's entry field when specifying a value. The next two code blocks provide the ability to rotate a sprite on its axis, clockwise and counterclockwise, as indicated by the direction of the arrow displayed on the blocks.

The following sample script demonstrates how to use the first two blocks to move a sprite around the stage in a clockwise manner.

This script executes whenever the green flag button is clicked. Once this event has occurred, four pairs of motion code blocks are executed at one-second intervals. This application uses the default cat sprite that is supplied as part of every new Scratch project. To create and test your own copy of the application, create a new Scratch application, click on the thumbnail of the cat sprite, drag it to the upper-left corner of the stage, and shrink it to about 50% of its normal size and then assemble the script.

The first two motion blocks in the script move the sprite 400 steps. Since the cat, by default, is pointed 90 degrees to the left, this will move the sprite from the upper-left corner of the stage to the upper-right corner of the stage. The next pair of motion blocks moves the sprite down to the bottom-right corner of the stage. The third pair of motion blocks moves the sprite to the bottom-left corner of the stage, and the last pair of motion blocks moves it back to the upper-left corner of the stage.

Note

All of the sprites supplied by Scratch have a predefined rotation axis. You can change the rotation axis for these sprites and set the rotation point for new sprites that you create or import into Scratch by editing the sprite using Scratch's Paint Editor program and then specifying a new rotation axis using the program's Set Rotation Point control.

A sprite's rotation is also affected by the selection of one of the three rotation buttons located on the left-hand side of the Sprite's info area. If you look at the cat sprite's rotation setting, you will see that the cat sprite is configured by default to rotate freely.

Figure 5.2 demonstrates the movements of the cat sprite as it moves from corner to corner, clockwise around the screen.

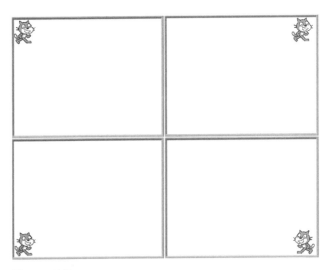

Figure 5.2
The cat's direction is changed by 90 degrees immediately after each move, readying it for its next move.

If you want, you can modify the script to move the sprite around the stage in a counterclockwise direction by modifying it, as demonstrated here:

Setting Sprite Direction

Scratch provides access to two motion blocks that can be used to point a sprite in a specified direction or to point a sprite towards the mouse-pointer or a specified sprite. These code blocks are shown in Figure 5.3.

The first of these blocks allows you to point a sprite in a particular direction as specified by the assignment of a numeric value representing the number of degrees that the sprite should be turned. You can either select a value of 0 = up, 90 = right, −90 = left, or 180 = down from the block's drop-down list or type in an integer value in the range of 0 to 360. For example, the following script demonstrates how to rotate a sprite 360 degrees, 90 degrees at a time at one-second intervals.

Figure 5.3
These code blocks can be used to point a sprite towards a specified direction or object.

Figure 5.4
An example of the four possible directions that the point in direction code block can point a sprite.

Figure 5.5
The cat rotates as necessary to continue facing the mouse-pointer.

This example uses the default cat sprite. Figure 5.4 shows an example of the four directions that the sprite turns when the script is executed. Note that for this example to work, you must click on the Can Rotate button in the sprite info area (allowing the sprite to rotate over a range of 360 degrees).

The second motion block shown in Figure 5.5 lets you point a sprite towards either the mouse-pointer or another sprite, as demonstrated in the following script.

In this example, the sprite is continuously repositioned so that is points towards the mouse-pointer. Therefore, whenever the mouse-pointer is moved around the stage, the image of the cat follows, as demonstrated in Figure 5.5.

N o t e

In order for the sprite shown in Figure 5.5 to continuously reposition itself, the motion block must be embedded within a control block that sets up a loop, repeatedly executing the motion block, allowing it to react every time the mouse-pointer is moved.

Repositioning a Sprite

Scratch provides access to three motion blocks that move a sprite to a specified coordination location on the stage, move a sprite to the location currently occupied by the mouse-pointer or another sprite, or move a sprite to a specified coordination position over a specified number of seconds. These code blocks are shown in Figure 5.6.

The first of these three motion blocks allows you to reposition a sprite to any location on the stage by specifying X-axis and Y-axis coordinates for the sprite. For example, the following script demonstrates how to reposition a sprite in the middle of the stage, pointing it in a 90-degree direction.

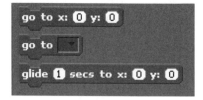

Figure 5.6
These code blocks can be used to move a sprite to a specific location.

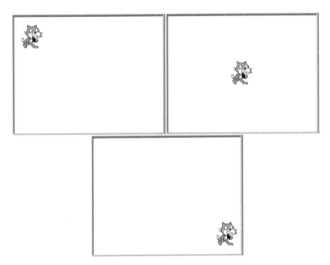

Figure 5.7
As this figure demonstrates, the sprite automatically moves around the stage, following the mouse-pointer.

The following script demonstrates how to move a sprite to the location on the stage currently occupied by the mouse-pointer.

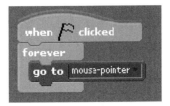

Figure 5.7 shows an example of the output that is generated when this script is run. If you look closely, you will see that in each of the three examples, the cat sprite remains positioned directly under the mouse-pointer no matter where it is moved on the stage.

This next script demonstrates how to reposition a sprite to a specific location on the stage. Instead of simply making the sprite appear at a specified location, as demonstrated in the previous two examples, this script repositions the sprite by moving or gliding to its new position in a smooth motion.

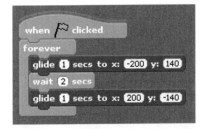

Changing Sprite Coordinates

Scratch provides four motion blocks that modify the location of a sprite on the stage either by assigning it new coordinates or by changing the sprite's coordinates by incrementing or decrementing their values. These code blocks are shown in Figure 5.8.

The following script demonstrates how to move a sprite across the stage in a series of eight steps. When first started, the script moves the sprite to the left-hand side of the stage, and then, using a loop, the sprite is moved by incrementing the value assigned to the X-axis coordinate by 50 and its Y-axis coordinate by -10 each time the loop repeats itself. As a result, the sprite is repeatedly repositioned and thus moved across the stage (in a descending angle over a period of eight seconds).

Bouncing Sprites Around the Stage

As a sprite is moved around the stage, it may eventually come into contact with one of the edges of the stage. Using the motion block shown next, you can instruct Scratch to bounce the sprite off of the edge of the stage.

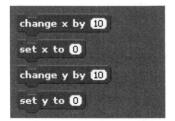

Figure 5.8
These code blocks provide the ability to modify a sprite's location by changing its coordinates.

The following script demonstrates how to use this code block to bounce a sprite around the stage:

This script reverses the direction that a sprite is traveling whenever it collides with the edge of the stage. If you were to add this script to the cat sprite in a new application, the cat would move across the stage from side to side until you halted the application's execution.

Keeping Track of Sprite Coordinates and Direction

Scratch provides three motion (reporter) blocks that can be used to retrieve and display information regarding the value of the sprite's X- and Y-coordinates as well as the sprite's direction. These code blocks are shown in Figure 5.9.

Note

Scratch's stage coordinate system allows for a coordinate range of -240 to 240 on its X-axis and a coordinate range of 180 to -180 on its Y-axis.

To set up an example that demonstrates how to work with these reporter blocks, create a new Scratch application and add the following script to the default cat sprite.

When executed, this script will move the cat sprite around the stage to wherever the mouse-pointer is located, bouncing it off the edge of the stage when necessary. After adding the script, select each of the reporter blocks by clicking on

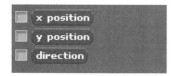

Figure 5.9
These code blocks provide the ability to retrieve and display a sprite's coordinates and direction.

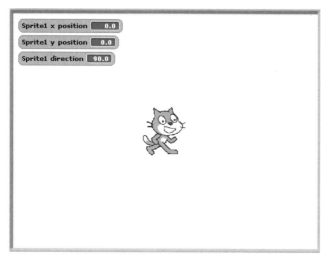

Figure 5.10
Displaying a sprite's coordinates and direction.

the check box just to the left of each block in the blocks palette. Once you have done this, three monitors should be visible on the stage, as demonstrated in Figure 5.10.

Once you have set up the application's monitors, run the application, move the mouse-pointer around the stage, and keep an eye on the values reported by the monitors.

Taking Advantage of Scratch Cards

One resource available to Scratch programmers is Scratch cards. *Scratch cards* are PDF files that you can print, cut out, glue together, and then use as a quick reference for performing certain tasks. You can download Scratch cards for free at http://scratch.wik.is/Support/Scratch_Cards, as shown in Figure 5.11.

The front of each Scratch card identifies the type of task that the card is designed to show you how to perform, and the back of the card provides detailed

Figure 5.11
Scratch cards serve as quick reference for performing specific types of tasks.

instruction on how to perform the task. As of the writing of this book, a dozen Scratch cards were available. The PDF file for each of these Scratch cards is descriptively named to identify the task that the card teaches you to perform. The list of available Scratch cards includes:

- Change Color
- Move to a Beat
- Key Moves
- Say Something
- Glide
- Follow the Mouse
- Dance Twist

- Interactive Whirl

- Animate It

- Moving Animation

- Surprise Button

- Keep Score

Figure 5.12 shows what the PDF file for the Key Moves Scratch card looks like. As you can see, the left-hand side of the Scratch card demonstrates the movement of

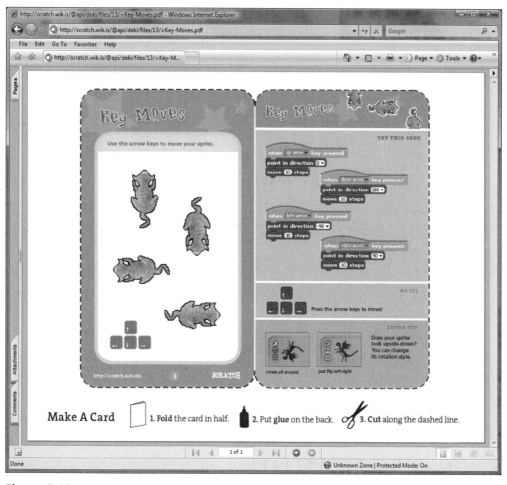

Figure 5.12
The Key Moves Scratch card demonstrates how to move a sprite around the stage using the keyboard arrow keys.

the sprite, and the right-hand side of the card provides an example of the code blocks needed to move the sprite in each of the four demonstrated directions. In addition, each Scratch card includes an extra tip that helps you further enhance the task being performed.

Tip

There are five Scratch cards that provide information specific to moving sprites around the stage. These Scratch cards are briefly described here:

- **Key Moves.** Demonstrates how to move a sprite around the stage using keyboard keys.

- **Move to a Beat.** Demonstrates how to create an animated dance sequence that moves to a drum beat.

- **Moving Animation.** Demonstrates how to animate the movements of a sprite using an alternative series of costumes.

- **Glide.** Demonstrates how to move a sprite around the stage from one point to another in a smooth motion.

- **Follow the Mouse.** Demonstrates how to script the movement of a sprite so that it follows the movement of the mouse-pointer on the stage.

Creating the Virtual Scratch Fish Tank

The rest of this chapter is dedicated to leading you through the development of a virtual fish tank application. In this Scratch application, five sprites, representing a range of colorful fish and a small octopus, busily swim around the fish tank, represented by a suitable background, as demonstrated in Figure 5.13.

This application will be created by following a series of steps, as outlined here:

1. Creating a new Scratch application project.

2. Adding a stage background.

3. Adding and removing sprites to and from the project.

4. Importing a sound file into the application.

5. Adding the programming logic required to play a background sound effect.

6. Adding the programming logic required to animate fish tank activity.

7. Saving and executing your work.

Figure 5.13
An example of the virtual fish tank application in action.

Step 1: Creating a New Scratch Project

The first step in creating this Scratch project is to start Scratch, thereby automatically creating a new Scratch application project. Alternatively, if you already have Scratch up and running, you can create a new project by clicking on the New button located on the Scratch menu bar.

Step 2: Adding a Background to the Stage

Once you have a new application project ready to go, let's begin by adding a suitable background to the stage that will give the virtual fish tank an appropriate look and feel. To set this up, click on the blank thumbnail representing the stage in the sprite list and then click on the Backgrounds tab located at the top of the scripts area. Next, click on the Import button, displaying the Import Background window. Double-click on the Nature folder, scroll down and select the underwater graphic, and then click on the OK button. Once the new background has been added, go ahead and remove the blank stage background from the application.

Step 3: Adding and Removing Sprites

The next step in the development of the virtual fish tank application is to add sprites to the application representing different marine life. Before doing this, remove the cat sprite from the application, since it is not needed. To do so,

Table 5.1 Sprite Rotational Buttons

Sprite Filename	Sprite Application Name
fish2	Purple
fish3	Yellow
fish4	Spotted
octopus1-a	Squid

right-click on its thumbnail in the sprites list and select Delete from the popup menu that appears. Once you have removed the cat sprite, it is time to add new sprites needed by the application.

In total, you need to add five new sprites. Four of the sprites will represent different fish, and the fifth sprite will represent a small octopus. To add the octopus sprite, click on the Choose Sprite from File button located in the middle of the new sprite button controls. This will open the New Sprite window. Double-click on the Animals folder, scroll down and select the fish1-a sprite, and then click on the OK button. Next, click on the sprite's thumbnail in the sprites area and then change the name assigned to the sprite to Blue.

Using the same set of steps described above, add the following list of sprites to the application project, renaming each sprite as indicated in Table 5.1.

Once you have added all five sprites, move the sprites to random locations on the stage. Next, change the direction in which each sprite moves by selecting each sprite and then changing it in the sprite info area by repositioning the direction of the blue line displayed on the image of the sprite.

Tip

To make the virtual fish tank more interesting, set the fish and the octopus up so that each moves in a different direction and angle.

Step 4: Adding a Suitable Audio File to the Stage

Now that the application's background and sprites have been added, it is time to add an audio file that when played will give the virtual fish tank a realistic feeling. Specifically, we'll add an audio file that when played makes bubble sounds. To accomplish this task, click on the thumbnail representing the stage in the sprite list and then click on the Sounds tab in the scripts area. Next, click on the Import button to display the Import Sound window. Next, double-click on the Effects folder and then select the Bubble audio file and click on OK.

Tip

To help keep your Scratch application as small as possible, remove the default pop audio file from the background.

Step 5: Playing the Audio File

Now it is time to add the programming logic needed to make your new application run. In total you will need to add six scripts to the project, one for the stage and one for each of the application's five sprites.

The script to be added to the stage will be responsible for playing the background sound effect that makes the virtual fish tank sound like a real fish tank. To create it, click on the stage thumbnail located in the sprites area and then select the Scripts tab located at the top of the scripts area. Next, add and configure the following code blocks exactly as shown here:

This script consists of a hat block that will execute whenever the green flag button is pressed. When this occurs, a loop is set up that repeatedly executes two blocks. The first code block is a sound block that plays the audio file you previously added to the stage. The second code block pauses script execution for four seconds to give Scratch time to finish playing the audio file, before allowing the loop to repeat and play it again.

Step 6: Animating the Swimming of the Fish

With the programming logic required to provide the application's background sound effect now in place, it is time to write the scripts that will animate the movement of the fish and octopus. To set this up, you need to add a small script to each of the sprites that provides the programming logic required to control the movement of the sprites as they move (or swim) around the fish tank.

Scripting the Movement of the Blue Fish

Let's begin by automating the movement of the sprite name Blue. Do so by clicking on the sprite's thumbnail and then creating the following script for it:

As you can see, this script is set up to begin executing the moment the user clicks on the green flag button. It contains a control block that sets up a loop that repeats the execution of two embedded motion blocks. The first motion block moves the sprite in its current direction every time the loop repeats. The second motion block tells Scratch to bounce the sprite off of the edge of the stage when reached. As a result, the sprite (blue fish) will appear to swim around the fish tank from side to side, and depending on whether you have adjusted its direction as instructed at the end of Step 3, it will move up and down as well.

Scripting the Movement of the Purple Fish

Next, let's create a script that controls the movement of the purple fish. Rather than build this script from scratch, let's take a shortcut. With the script for the blue fish currently displayed on the scripts area, drag and drop the script onto the thumbnail representing the purple sprite in the sprites list. This adds an exact copy of the script to the purple sprite, which you can then view and modify by clicking on the purple sprite's thumbnail.

To make things interesting, modify the number of steps that the purple sprite is moved from 1 to 2, as shown here:

Other than moving the purple fish at a little faster pace than the blue fish, the programming logic that controls both fish is identical. In fact, the programming for all of the remaining fish and the octopus is identical, except for variances in the number of steps the sprites are moved.

Scripting the Movement of the Yellow Fish

Using drag and drop, add a copy of the purple sprite's script to the yellow sprite and then modify it as shown here:

As you can see, the yellow sprite has been configured to move at the same pace as the blue sprite.

Scripting the Movement of the Spotted Fish

Once again, using drag and drop, add a copy of the yellow sprite's script to the spotted sprite and then modify it as shown here:

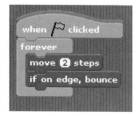

This time the sprite has been configured so that it moves two steps at a time.

Scripting the Movement of the Octopus

Last but not least, drag and drop the script for the spotted sprite onto the sprite representing the octopus and then modify it as shown here:

As you can see, this sprite has been configured to move slower than any of the other sprites, at just a half step at a time.

Step 7: Saving and Executing Your New Scratch Application

At this point your copy of the virtual fish tank application should be complete and should look like the example shown in Figure 5.14.

If you have not done so yet, save your new application and then run it to see how it looks. To save your application, click on the Save button located on the Scratch menu bar. This will display the Save Project window, allowing you to specify the name of the application, the location where you want to store it, your name, and comments documenting the application and its purpose.

Figure 5.14
The completed application consists of a background, five sprites, and six scripts.

Once you have saved your application, go ahead and run it. Since all of the scripts in the application are configured to execute when the green flag button is pressed, all you have to do is to click on the green flag button and then sit back and relax as you watch and listen to your virtual fish tank.

Summary

This chapter taught you how to work with all 16 motion code blocks. You learned how to move and rotate sprites, point sprites in different directions or towards different objects, and change a sprite's location. You also learned how to control whether a sprite jumps to its new location or glides to it, how to change a sprite's location by setting or modifying the value of its X-axis and Y-axis coordinates, how to control a sprite's movement when it makes contact with the edge of the stage, and how to report on a sprite's position and direction. You also learned how to work with Scratch cards and create a virtual fish tank application.

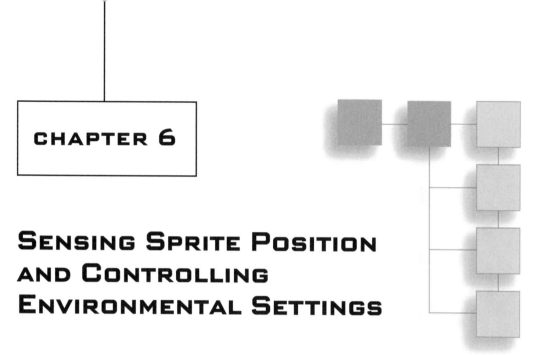

CHAPTER 6

SENSING SPRITE POSITION AND CONTROLLING ENVIRONMENTAL SETTINGS

To create many interactive computer applications, you need the ability to detect when certain things are happening. For example, in a car racing game, it would be important to be able to detect when two cars (sprites) bump into one another, and in a game that uses predefined keystrokes as input for controlling certain game functions, you need to be able to detect when those keys have been pressed. Scratch provides the ability to detect or sense when things happen using sensing code blocks. This chapter will demonstrate how to work with various sensing blocks and will also guide you through the creation of a new Scratch application, the Family Scrapbook.

The major topics covered in this chapter include learning how to

- Detect mouse-pointer location and mouse button status

- Detect when keyboard keys are pressed

- Determine when a sprite collides with other objects on the stage

- Keep track of a sprite's distance from other objects and retrieve different sprite properties

- Work with a timer and detect the loudness of microphone input

Working with Sensing Code Blocks

An important capability needed by a graphical programming language that works with sprites is the ability to determine when certain things happen. For example, sprite-based applications typically need to know when sprites collide with one another or when the user presses certain keystrokes. This type of functionality is provided in Scratch by sensing blocks.

Sensing blocks also provide the ability to determine the location of the mouse-pointer and the ability to determine a sprite's distance from other sprites. Sensing blocks are colored sky blue. In total, Scratch provides access to 15 different sensing blocks, which you can work with by clicking on the Sensing button located at the top of the blocks palette.

Scratch organizes sensing blocks into eight sub-groupings, each of which is separated by a blank space in the blocks palette. These sub-groupings include:

- Sensing blocks that retrieve and report on the left mouse button status and mouse-pointer coordinates.

- A sensing block that determines when specified keyboard keys have been pressed.

- Sensing blocks that determine if a sprite has made contact with the mouse-pointer, another sprite, or the edge of the stage.

- A sensing block that reports on a sprite's distance from the mouse-pointer or another sprite.

- Sensing blocks that provide access to a built-in timer that can be used to control the timing of application activity.

- A sensing block that retrieves a property value (X position, Y position, direction, costume number, size, or volume) for the stage or a specified sprite.

- Sensing blocks that report on how loud audio input coming from the computer's microphone is.

- Sensing blocks that work with a Scratch Board, allowing you to create applications that can detect changes in light and sound and work with the Scratch Board's buttons and slider control.

Except for the `reset timer` code block, all sensing code blocks are reporter blocks, designed to be embedded inside stack blocks. Examples of how to work with each of the sensing code blocks listed above are provided throughout the rest of this chapter.

Retrieving Mouse Button and Coordinate Status

In many types of applications, the mouse-pointer is used to control the movement of sprites and to affect the operation of the application in many other different ways. The sensing blocks shown in Figure 6.1 provide access to data about the operation of the mouse-pointer.

The first of these three code blocks retrieves the location of the mouse-pointer as it moves along the X-axis. As was stated in Chapter 2, "Getting Comfortable with the Scratch Development Environment," Scratch supports a total range of –240 to 240. The second of these code blocks retrieves the location of the mouse-pointer as it moves along the Y-axis. Scratch supports a total range of 180 to –180 on its Y-axis. The third code block is used to retrieve a true/false value that identifies when the mouse's button is being pressed. The following script, which is part of a drawing application, demonstrates how to work with all three of these sensing code blocks.

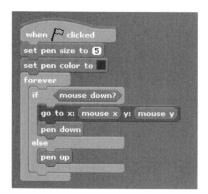

Figure 6.1
These sensing blocks report on the mouse-pointer's coordinates and button status.

To create the drawing application, create a new Scratch application project. Remove the cat sprite from it and then create and add a new sprite that consists of a single black dot. Next, select the thumbnail representing the dot and then add the script shown above to it.

This application's operation depends on the use of a virtual pen object that Scratch makes available to you via pen code blocks, which you will learn about in Chapter 12, "Drawing Lines and Shapes." The overall operation of the application is controlled by the script, which automatically begins executing when the green flag button is clicked. Once started, two pen blocks are used to set the width of the pen and the color used by the pen when drawing. Next, a forever code block has been added to repeat the execution of all the code blocks embedded within it.

Within the loop, an if...else code block is used to conditionally control the execution of three additional statements. The if...else code block's execution is controlled by examining the value returned by a sensing block that returns a value of true when the user presses the mouse's left button and false if the mouse's left button is not being pressed.

When the user presses the left mouse button, the two statements located at the top of the if...else code block are executed. The first statement moves the sprite to the same location as the pointer, and the second code block places Scratch's virtual pen in a down position, allowing drawing to begin. As a result, a blue line is drawn anywhere on the stage where the mouse-pointer is moved when the left mouse button is being pressed. The code block located at the bottom of the if...else code block is executed whenever the user releases the left mouse button, lifting the virtual pen and halting any drawing operations.

Figure 6.2 demonstrates the operation of the drawing application.

Figure 6.2
An example of the drawing application in action.

Determining when Keys Are Pressed

One problem with the drawing application is that there is no way to clear the screen and start over should you make a mistake when drawing. This can be easily rectified using the sensing code block shown in Figure 6.3, which retrieves a true or false, depending on whether a specified key is pressed.

To see an example of how to work with this code block, let's modify the previous drawing application by editing the script belonging to the application's sprite, as shown here.

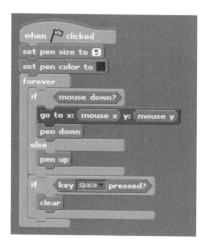

As you can see, three new code blocks have been added that clear the stage whenever the spacebar is pressed. Figure 6.4 shows an example of the drawing application in operation. Here, the application is used to draw the name Lee on the stage. Next, the spacebar is pressed, clearing the stage, after which an image of a tree has been drawn.

Figure 6.3
This sensing block can be used to detect when the user presses a specified keyboard key.

Figure 6.4
This enhanced version of the drawing application can be used to draw and erase.

Tip

In addition to detecting keystrokes using a sensing code block, you can also use the control code block shown in Figure 6.5. The difference between these two code blocks is that the sensing code block can be used within a loop to continuously determine that a specified keyboard key is being pressed. The control block, on the other hand, only executes once when the specified key is initially pressed and is therefore good for initiating an individual action and not for facilitating the repeated execution of an action. You will learn more about this code block later in Chapter 9, "Conditional and Repetitive Logic."

Figure 6.5
This code block is used to initiate an action whenever a specific keyboard key is pressed.

Determining when Sprites Collide with Other Objects

One key programming requirement of many computer games is the ability to determine when a sprite collides with another sprite, the edge of the screen, or the mouse-pointer. Scratch provides the ability to perform collision detection using the three sensing code blocks shown in Figure 6.6.

The first code block shown in Figure 6.6 can be used to determine when a sprite makes contact with a specified sprite, the edge of the stage, or the mouse-pointer. The list of objects that this code block can detect is accessible in the block's drop-down list. As an example of how to work with this code block, modify the previous Scratch application by replacing its script with the one shown here.

This script demonstrates how to determine when a sprite comes into contact with the edge of the stage. This script executes whenever the green flag button is clicked and uses a `forever` block to set up a loop that repeatedly executes all embedded code blocks. Within the loop, you'll find a conditional `if` block that executes embedded statements when the mouse's left-button is being pressed.

Figure 6.6
These sensing blocks can be used to look for collisions.

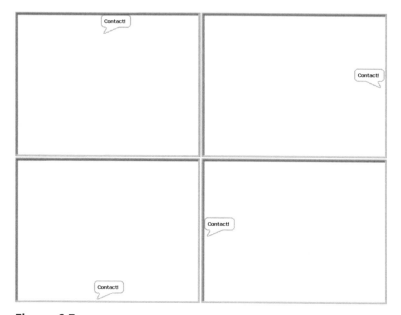

Figure 6.7
An example of the text that is displayed whenever the sprite makes contact with the edge of the stage.

When this is the case, a motion block is used to make the application's sprite follow the mouse-pointer around the stage. A second sensing code block is used within another conditional if code block to detect when the sprite makes contact with the edge of the stage. When this occurs, a looks code block is executed, displaying a text message in a voice bubble.

Figure 6.7 demonstrates the output that is displayed when you rerun the application with this new script and move the mouse-pointer to one of the edges of the stage.

Next, let's take a look at an example of how to work with the second sensing block shown in Figure 6.7. This code block can be used to detect when a sprite makes contact with a specific color on the stage. To see a working example of how to work with this code block, create a new Scratch application and then create and add a new sprite in the shape of a red rectangle (using the Paint Editor), placing it

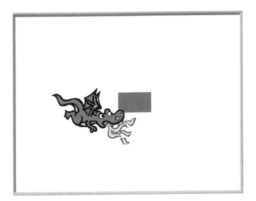

Figure 6.8
This red square will be used to demonstrate the ability to detect a collision with a specific color on the stage.

in the middle of the stage. Next, add a second sprite to the application by clicking on the Choose New Sprite from File button, opening the New Sprite window. Next, drill down into the Fantasy folder and select the dragon1-b sprite and then click on OK. The stage for your new application should now look like the example shown in Figure 6.8.

Next, add the following script belonging to the sprite representing the dragon. When executed, this script plays an audio file whenever the sprite is moved into contact with the red square in the center of the stage.

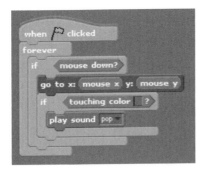

Note that to correctly set the color specification in the sensing block, you must click on the color block embedded within the control. This displays a small eyedropper graphic that you can then move to the area on the stage that contains the color you want to detect. Click on that color, and Scratch will automatically change the code block's color to match the color that you clicked on.

At this point you should have everything set up and ready to run. Go ahead and run the application and then press and hold the left mouse button and move the mouse-pointer on and off of the red rectangle in the middle of the stage and listen for the audio file to be played.

Using the previous code block, you can set up an application to detect a collision any time any part of a sprite comes into contact with a specific color on the stage. In the previous example, this occurs whenever any part of the dragon sprite (head, tail, wings, flames, etc.) comes into contact with the red rectangle sprite.

However, if you prefer, you can use the third sensing code clock shown in Figure 6.6 to set up a more specific type of collision test. Specifically, what this code block does is allow you to specify a color on the sprite that must make contact with another color on the stage for a collision to occur. To get a better understanding of the difference between this code block and the previous sensing code block, look at the following script.

The following script demonstrates how to use the second of these sensing blocks in a script that plays an audio file whenever a specified color within a sprite comes into contact with a specified color on the stage.

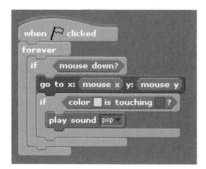

In this example, the sensing code block has been replaced. Now, for a collision to occur, the yellow color on the sprite must come into contact with the red color on the stage. If you were to replace the script in the previous application with this script, then the only time a collision will occur is when the yellow flames coming out of the dragon's mouth touch the red rectangle sprite, as demonstrated in Figure 6.9.

Determining Distance

Rather than detecting when one sprite collides with another sprite, you may want to detect when one sprite comes within a certain distance of another sprite or the mouse-pointer. You can do this using the sensing code block shown in Figure 6.10.

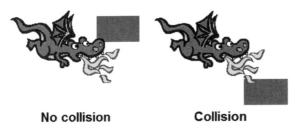

No collision   **Collision**

Figure 6.9
Setting up a more restrictive collision test.

Figure 6.10
This sensing block reports on a sprite's distance from a specified object.

To develop an understanding of how to work with this code block, modify the previous Scratch application, replacing the dragon sprite's script with the script shown here.

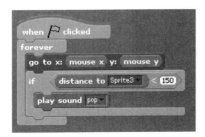

One you have replaced the script, run the application and then move the mouse-pointer around the stage. When you do, the dragon sprite will follow, and whenever it moves within 150 steps of the red rectangle sprite, an audio file will be repeatedly played.

Working with a Timer

Another pair of sensing code blocks that you need to become familiar with is shown in Figure 6.11. These code blocks provide the ability to enable and work with Scratch's built-in timer.

The first code block resets the timer back to its default value of zero, and the second code block retrieves a number specifying how many seconds have passed since the timer started running. Using Scratch's timer, you can control the pace

Figure 6.11
These sensing blocks provide the ability to enable and use a timer within your Scratch application.

of animation and the operation of your Scratch applications. For example, you would need to use these controls to keep track of time when players are given a certain amount of time in which to make a move.

The following example demonstrates how to use both of these timer code blocks to create a script that repeatedly plays an audio file for five seconds.

Retrieving Stage and Sprite Data

In addition to determining mouse status, sprite collisions, and the distance between sprites, you can use the code block shown in Figure 6.12 to retrieve sprite and stage information.

This code block provides easy access to a number of pieces of information, including:

- X position
- Y position
- Direction
- Costume number
- Size
- Volume

Figure 6.12
This sensing block can be used to retrieve information about a number of object attributes.

As an example of how to work with this code block, take a look at the following script, which retrieves the X coordinate of a sprite named Sprite 2 and plays an audio file whenever that sprite is moved to the right-hand side of the stage (between coordinates 1 and 240).

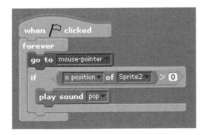

Retrieving Audio Data

In addition to sensing mouse-pointer and keyboard data, collisions, distance, and other stage and sprite properties and working with the timer, Scratch also provides access to a pair of sensing blocks, shown in Figure 6.13, that allow you to sense sound input from the computer's microphone (if it has one) and to use that input within your Scratch applications.

The first of these two sensing blocks retrieves a number, from 1 to 100, representing the volume of the computer's microphone, and the second code block retrieves a true/false value, depending on whether a sound value of 30 or greater is detected through the computer's microphone.

The following example demonstrates how to create a script that plays an audio file named pop whenever a loud sound is detected through the computer's microphone.

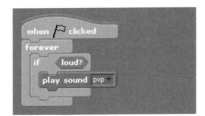

Figure 6.13
These sensing blocks are used to report on how loud a sound is being played.

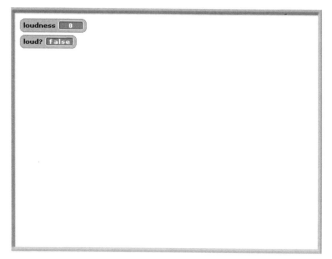

Figure 6.14
Using monitors to keep track of the loudness of audio playback and input.

Both of the code blocks shown in Figure 6.13 are monitor blocks, so if you want, you can display their results on the stage, as demonstrated in Figure 6.14.

Code Blocks That Work with Sensor Boards

Scratch supplies additional sensing code blocks, as shown in Figure 6.15. In order to work with these code blocks, you need a Scratch Board. A *Scratch Board* is a special piece of hardware that you can buy from the Scratch website and then attach to your computer. You can use the Scratch Board to collect and process different environmental and user-provided input.

The first of these two blocks retrieves the value reported by one of the sensors on a Scratch Board. The second code block retrieves a Boolean value of true or false, depending on whether a specified sensor is being pressed. Learning how to work with a Scratch Board is outside of the scope of this chapter. Instead, you will learn

Figure 6.15
These sensing blocks are used in conjunction with a Scratch Board.

how to programmatically interact with and control Scratch Boards in Chapter 14, "Collecting External Input Using a Scratch Board."

Creating the Family Scrapbook Application

The remainder of this chapter will guide you through the development of your next Scratch application, an electronic family scrapbook. In total, this application will consist of one sprite, a blank stage, and three scripts. Once created, you can use this application to display any number of electronic photographs in an automated photo album that displays pictures at three-second intervals. Each picture in the application is actually just a costume added to the application's sprite. Figures 6.16 and 6.17 show how the application looks when displaying two of the photo book's pictures.

The development of this application project will be created by following a series of steps, as outlined here:

1. Creating a new Scratch application project.

2. Adding and removing sprites and costumes.

3. Importing a sound file into the application.

4. Adding the programming logic required to play background music.

5. Adding the programming logic required to manage the display of photographs.

6. Saving and executing your work.

Step 1: Creating a New Scratch Project

The first step in creating the Family Scrapbook project is to create a new Scratch application project. Do so either by opening Scratch, thereby automatically creating a new Scratch application project, or by clicking on the New button located on the Scratch menu bar.

Figure 6.16
An example of one of the sprite's costumes.

Figure 6.17
Another example of one of the sprite's costumes.

Step 2: Adding and Removing Sprites and Costumes

This application consists of a single sprite, which will be used to display all of the application's photographs (as costumes). Therefore, the default cat sprite will not be needed and should be removed. After removing the cat sprite, click on the Choose New Sprite from File button to open the New Sprite window. Using this window, navigate to the folder containing the electronic image files (photographs) that you plan on displaying, and then select one of these files to be used as the application's sprite.

Click on the thumbnail representing the new sprite (in the sprites list) and then click on the Costumes tab located at the top of the scripts area. Next, click on the

Figure 6.18
You can add as many pictures as you want to the sprite's list of costumes.

Import button, opening the Import Costume window. Using this window, add another picture to the application. Repeat this process as many times as necessary to add all of the image files that you want to be included as part of the family scrapbook, as demonstrated in Figure 6.18.

Step 3: Adding a Suitable Audio File to the Stage

To make the Family Scrapbook application more enjoyable, let's add a little background music to help set the mood. To add the music file, select the stage thumbnail in the sprites list and then click on the Sounds tab located at the top of the scripts area. Next, click on the Import button to display the Import Sound window and then double-click on the Music Loops folder and then select the GuitarChords1 audio file and click on OK, adding the sound file to the application project, as shown in Figure 6.19.

Figure 6.19
Adding background music to be played when the application executes.

Step 4: Playing the Audio File

The next step in the development of the application project is to begin adding the programming logic. In total, you will need to add three scripts to the project, one for the stage and two for the application's sprite.

The script to be added to the stage will be responsible for playing the application's background music. To create this script, click on the stage thumbnail located in the sprites list and then select the Scripts tab located at the top of the scripts area. Next, add and configure the following code blocks exactly as shown here.

This script manages the repeated playback of the application's audio file for as long as the application is run. Audio file playback is performed using a pair of sound blocks, which you will learn about in Chapter 11, "Spicing Things Up with Sounds."

Step 5: Displaying the Photographs

Now it is time to add the programming logic that is responsible for displaying all of the photographs that make up the Family Scrapbook. To set this up, you need to add a small script to the application's sprite that specifies the programming logic required to automate the display of all of the application's photographs, at three-second intervals. In addition, you will add a second script to the application that will allow the user to manually control the display of the application's photographs.

Scripting the Operation of the Family Scrapbook

The code blocks that are responsible for automating the operation of the scrapbook are shown here:

This script is automatically executed when the user clicks on the green flag button. When this happens, a looks block is executed. This block specifies a specific costume to be displayed when the application is first started (the first costume in the costume list). Next, a loop is set up that repeatedly executes the two statements embedded within it. The first code block located inside the loop pauses the script's execution for three seconds, after which a second looks block is used to switch the sprite's costume to the next costume in the sprite's costume list.

Allowing for the Manual Operation of the Family Scrapbook

If the user prefers, rather than viewing photographs in the Family Scrapbook as an automated slideshow, the contents of the scrapbook can be manually browsed by clicking on the application's sprite, which causes the next costume (photograph) to be displayed. To provide the user with this manual option, add the following script to the application's sprite.

Step 6: Saving and Executing Your New Scratch Application

Okay, assuming that you have been following along and creating your copy of the Family Scrapbook application as you made your way through this chapter, then your copy of the Family Scrapbook application should look something like the example shown in Figure 6.20.

Figure 6.20
The completed application consists of a blank stage and a single sprite with 11 costumes and two scripts.

So, if you have not done so yet, save your new application by clicking on the Save button located on the Scratch menu bar. This will display the Save Project window, allowing you to name the application and specify the location where you want to store it. Once saved, switch to Presentation mode, click on the green flag button, and kick back and enjoy listening to and watching your new application. Alternatively, start clicking on the application's sprite and go through the contents of the Family Scrapbook at your own pace.

Summary

This chapter has provided a review of all of the Scratch sensing code blocks (except for the ones that work with Scratch Boards). You learned how to detect collisions, identify when the left mouse button or a keyboard key is pressed, and even to determine when a sprite comes into contact with different colors on the stage. You learned how to work with the timer as a means of controlling application activity. This chapter also showed you how to retrieve different property values belonging to sprites and the stage and to detect the loudness of microphone input. Use of the information presented in this chapter is key to the development of interactive Scratch applications and games.

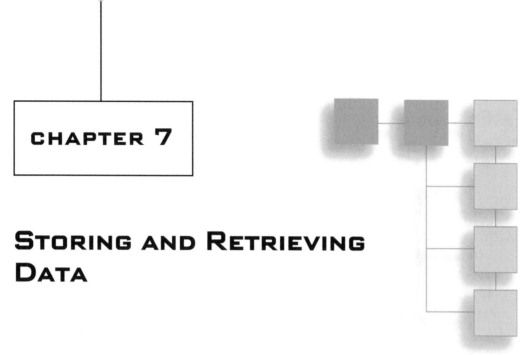

CHAPTER 7

STORING AND RETRIEVING DATA

All computer applications require some sort of data with which to work as they execute. This is true of even the simplest applications. The data processed by an application may be embedded within it. Data may also be randomly generated or collected from the user as the application executes. In order to work with and manipulate data, programmers need the ability to store, retrieve, and modify data when an application runs. Within Scratch applications, data is managed using variables. The goal of this chapter is to teach you everything you need to know to begin developing Scratch applications that can collect, store, and process application data.

The major topics covered in this chapter include:

- How to create local and global variables

- How to use variables as a means of storing and retrieving data

- How to delete variables that are no longer needed

- How to view data stored in local variables belonging to other sprites

Learning How to Work with Application Data

Like all computer programs, Scratch applications need to be able to process and store data. *Data* is any type of information that your Scratch applications collect, process, and store when executing. Data can also be collected when the user

Figure 7.1
An example of text embedded within a looks code block.

interacts with the application using the keyboard or mouse. Data may be generated by your applications such as when you create a Scratch project that generates and then uses random numbers (covered in Chapter 8). Data may also be hard-coded within your Scratch application projects. For example, the code block shown in Figure 7.1 can be used to store and display a text string within a script.

When executed, a script containing this looks code block will display the hard-coded text string inside a voice bubble. Like most programming languages, Scratch lets you work with a number of different types of data. Each of these different types of data, listed next, is handled differently by Scratch.

- String

- Boolean

- Integer

- Real

A *string* is a piece of text data that you hard code within Scratch applications using different types of looks code blocks, which you will learn how to work with in Chapter 10, "Changing the Way Sprites Look and Behave." Boolean data is data that is automatically generated by Scratch when you work with different types of numbers code blocks (which you will learn about in Chapter 8). A *Boolean* value represents data that has an assigned value of either True or False. For example, any time you compare one numeric value against another to see if they are equal, Scratch returns a Boolean value. Based on the result of that analysis, you can alter the way your Scratch applications execute using control blocks, which are covered in Chapter 9, "Conditional and Repetitive Logic."

An *integer* is a numeric value that does not include a decimal point (sometimes referred to as a whole number). Scratch lets you enter integer values as input into numerous different types of code blocks. It also allows you to store numeric data inside variables, allowing you to store, retrieve, and manipulate the data as necessary during application execution. A *real* number is a number that includes a decimal number.

Scratch handles different types of data differently. For example, string data can only be displayed by embedding it within looks code blocks. Integer and real data can also be embedded within code blocks and displayed in monitors. In addition, integer and real data can be added, subtracted, and manipulated in all the different ways that you would to be able to manipulate numeric data. Scratch also allows you to use integers and real numbers interchangeably.

Note

Industrial strength programming languages Microsoft C++ and Visual Basic support a much wider range of data types. However, they all support the same basic types of data that Scratch does.

Storing Data in Variables

As has already been stated, you can embed numeric data inside different types of code blocks, using it to control the operation of scripts. You can also store numeric data collected when your applications execute using variables. In Scratch, *variables* allow you to store, retrieve, and modify numeric data.

Note

Scratch cannot store string or Boolean data in variables.

Creating Scratch Variables

In order to store, modify, and retrieve data in a Scratch application, you need to create variables. In order to work with variables within your Scratch applications, you must first define and add them to your application projects. This is done by clicking on the Variables button located at the top of the blocks palette and then clicking on the Make a Variable button, as shown in Figure 7.2.

Once this button has been clicked, Scratch displays the window shown in Figure 7.3, allowing you to assign a name to the variable.

Figure 7.2
Creating and deleting Scratch variables.

Figure 7.3
Assigning a name to a new Scratch variable.

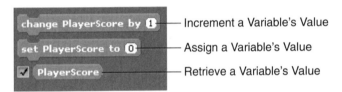

Figure 7.4
Scratch creates three new code blocks for each variable that you create.

Figure 7.5
Every new variable supports a monitor that displays its value.

The name that you assign will be used to create and add three new code blocks to your Scratch project, as shown in Figure 7.4.

In addition, a monitor showing the variable's value is automatically displayed on the stage, as demonstrated in Figure 7.5.

Using the three code blocks created for every variable, you can assign an initial value to the variable, change its value while your application is running, and display a monitor on the stage, which shows the variable's value.

Assigning Variables to Sprites and the Stage

Variables in Scratch applications belong to the sprites in which they are defined (or to the stage). Therefore, it is important that when adding new variables to your application, you select the thumbnail for the sprite (or stage) where the variable belongs. For example, variables that need to be accessed by different scripts belonging to different sprites may best be added to the stage, whereas a variable needed only by a specific sprite should be added to that sprite.

Assigning Names to Your Variables

Unlike many programming languages, Scratch is very flexible when it comes to naming variables. You can make variable names as long or as short as you want. Variable names can include:

- Letters

- Numbers

- Special characters

- Blank spaces

Because Scratch creates an endless supply of code blocks for each new variable that you define, it eliminates any concerns about case-sensitivity, making things a lot easier to work with.

Tip

Make your variable names as descriptive as possible. This will help make your scripts self-documenting. Although Scratch variable names can be extremely long, it's a good idea to limit their length to a maximum of 30 characters. This provides you with plenty of room to create descriptive, manageable variable names.

Understanding Variable Scope

One very important concept that you need to understand when working with variables is *variable scope*. A variable's scope identifies the location within an application where the variable's value can be modified. Scratch supports two levels of variable scope, as outlined here:

- **Local.** Variables that can be modified only by scripts belonging to the sprite in which the variable is defined.

- **Global.** Variables that can be modified by any script in an application.

Note

Although local variables can only be modified by scripts belonging to the sprite in which they are defined, their assigned values can be retrieved (not modified) by scripts belonging to other sprites using sensing code blocks, as demonstrated a little later in this chapter.

Figure 7.6
Creating a local variable named `Counter`.

Creating Local Variables

Local variables can be modified only within the sprite in which they are defined. The following procedure outlines the steps involved in creating a local variable.

1. Select the sprite (or stage) to which the variable is to be added.

2. Click on the Variables button located at the top of the blocks palette.

3. Click on the Make a Variable button.

4. Enter the name you want to assign to the variable and then select the For This Sprite Only option, as demonstrated in Figure 7.6.

Since a local variable can only be modified within the sprite to which it has been added, it cannot be modified by scripts belonging to other sprites. If you need a variable that can be accessed by any script within an application, create a global variable as discussed in the next section.

Creating Global Variables

Unlike local variables, a global variable's value can be modified by any script within the application where it has been defined. You use the exact same procedure to create a global variable as you do when creating a local variable, the only difference being that you need to leave the default For All Sprites option selected when naming your variable, as demonstrated in Figure 7.7.

Tip

It is considered a good programming practice to restrict the scope of all variables to local whenever possible. This helps to make your applications easier to maintain and eliminates the possibility that you might accidentally modify the variable's value using scripts belonging to other sprites.

Figure 7.7
Creating a global variable named `Total Score`.

Figure 7.8
Deleting a variable that is no longer needed.

Deleting Variables when They Are No Longer Needed

Over time, you may find yourself making numerous changes to your Scratch projects. As you do, you may find that certain variables are no longer needed by your applications. If this is the case, you can clean up your applications by deleting these variables from your projects. Doing so is very easy: First, make sure that any references to the variable within the application's scripts have been removed and then click on the Delete a Variable button, as demonstrated in Figure 7.8, and select the variable that you want to delete. In response, Scratch will delete the variable from the sprite to which it was added.

Caution

> If you delete a variable from a sprite without first removing references to the variable in the sprite's scripts, Scratch will delete the variable but will also leave in place any code blocks in the application's scripts that reference that variable. As a result, things will not work properly.

Accessing Variables Belonging to Other Sprites

Although data stored in local variables can only be changed by scripts belonging to the sprite to which the variables have been assigned, Scratch does allow scripts belonging to other sprites to view data stored in variables belonging to other sprites. To view data stored in another sprite's local variables, you need to use the sensing block shown in Figure 7.9.

Figure 7.9
Using this code block, you can create a script that can view data stored in another sprite's local variables.

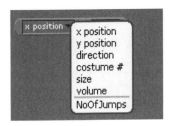

Figure 7.10
Specifying the name of the sprite whose variable you want to access.

Figure 7.11
Selecting the variable whose data you want to access.

This code block lets one sprite retrieve another sprite's X position, Y position, direction, costume number, size, and volume. It also lets you retrieve values assigned to another sprite's variable. As demonstrated in Figure 7.10, you can click on the code block's right-hand pull-down menu, and it will display a listing made up of the stage and all of the sprites in the Scratch application.

After selecting the stage or a sprite, you can use the drop-down menu located on the left-hand side of the code block to select and retrieve information for any of the specified items that are listed. A gray horizontal divider bar located at the bottom of the resulting list denotes the sprite's list of variables, separating the list from other available data, as demonstrated in Figure 7.11.

Using this code block, you can retrieve data stored in any sprite's local variables. However, all you can do is read the value assigned to those variables; you cannot modify them. The only variables that can be remotely modified are global variables.

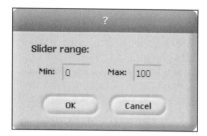

Figure 7.12
Configuring the upper and lower limits of a variable's slider control.

Working with Variable Monitors

As you learned back in Chapter 3, "A Review of the Basic Components of Scratch Projects," Scratch supports the display of monitors for many of its code blocks, including variable code blocks. In addition to being able to display a variable's value in either normal or large readout, variable monitors also support a third slider bar monitor format. To display a slider bar for any variable, enable the display of the variable's monitor and then right-click on the resulting monitor and select the Slider option from the popup menu that is displayed.

Sliders have a small round handle on them that you can drag to modify the value assigned to a variable. By default, you can use the slider to assign a value in the range of 1 to 100 to its variable, although you can assign any value to the variable by keying it into the code block's input field. If you need to, Scratch will let you change a slider bar's range by right-clicking on it and selecting the Set Slider Min and Max option from the popup menu that is displayed. When you do this, the window shown in Figure 7.12 displays, allowing you to specify any range you want.

Two Quick Examples

To help you become more comfortable with working with variables, let's look at two quick examples. In the first example, shown next, a script has been created that when executed will display the value assigned to a variable named Counter. Remember, by default every variable that you create has a reporter block with an associated monitor, which Scratch displays by default on the stage.

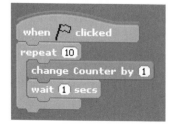

Note

To set up and run this example, you must create a new application and add a variable named Counter to it and then add the script to the application's default script.

This script has been set up to execute whenever the green flag button is pressed. It uses a control block to set up a loop that repeats the execution of two embedded code blocks a total of 10 times. Each time the loop executes, the value assigned to a variable named Counter is increased by 1. The next statement pauses the loop for one second before allowing it to continue running.

By default, Scratch assigns a default value of zero to all new variables, which is why the first time you run the previous script, it counts from 1 to 10. However, if you run it again, you will notice that it will count from 11 to 20. If you want, you can change this behavior by explicitly assigning an initial value to the Counter variable, as demonstrated in the following example:

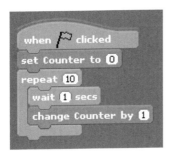

Here, the value of Counter has been set to 0 through the addition of a new variable block at the beginning of the script, immediately after its hat code block. As a result, no matter how many times this script executes, it always counts from 1 to 10.

Developing the Basketball Quiz Project

The rest of this chapter is devoted to guiding you through the development of your next Scratch application, the NBA Trivia Quiz. This application makes extensive use of variables to store and retrieve player input and to keep track of the player's quiz results. In total, the application is made up of a background, six sprites, and six scripts.

When executed, this application presents the user with an electronic quiz made up of five questions, designed to evaluate the user's knowledge of NBA trivia.

Figure 7.13 shows an example of how the game looks when first started. To begin game play, the user must click on the sprite representing the game's hostess, at which point she will begin administering the quiz.

Figure 7.14 provides an example of how the hostess interacts with the user when administering the quiz.

The hostess provides the user with immediate feedback after each question is answered, letting the user know if the answer was correct or incorrect. In addition, the user's score is automatically tabulated after each answer is evaluated and displayed in a monitor located at the lower right-hand side of the stage.

Figure 7.13
The NBA Trivia Quiz presents the user with a series of multiple choice questions.

Figure 7.14
The user answers questions by clicking on buttons labeled A, B, C, and D located on the right-hand side of the stage.

The development of this application project will be created by following a series of steps, as outlined here:

1. Creating a new Scratch application project.

2. Adding a background to the stage.

3. Adding and removing sprites and costumes.

4. Adding variables needed by the application.

5. Adding scripts to each button sprite to collect user answers.

6. Adding the programming logic required to administer the quiz.

7. Saving and executing your work.

Step 1: Creating a New Scratch Project

The first step in creating the NBA Trivia Quiz application is to create a new Scratch application project. Do so by starting Scratch, thereby automatically creating a new Scratch application project or, if Scratch is already running, by clicking on the New button located on the Scratch menu bar.

Step 2: Selecting an Appropriate Stage Background

Once you have created your new Scratch project, it is time to get to work. Let's begin by adding an appropriate background to the stage. To do so, click on the blank stage thumbnail located in the sprite list. Once selected, modify its background by clicking on the Backgrounds tab located at the top of the scripts area. To add a new background to the application, click on the Import button. When the Import Background window opens, click on the Indoors folder and then select the basketball-court thumbnail and click on the OK button.

Since this application only requires one background, you can remove the default blank background named background1 from your project by clicking on its Delete This Costume button.

Step 3: Adding and Removing Sprites

This application consists of a number of sprites, representing a hostess who is responsible for administering the quiz, four buttons on which the user must click when answering quiz questions, and a graphic containing a welcoming text message. Before adding any sprites, go ahead and remove the cat sprite from the application, since it will not be needed.

To add the sprite representing the game's hostess, click on the Choose New Sprite from File button to open the New Sprite window. Drill down in to the People folder and then select the `girl3-standing` sprite and click on the OK button. Enlarge the sprite and reposition it as demonstrated in Figures 7.13 and 7.14. While you are at it, change the name assigned to the sprite to say host.

Next, click on the Choose New Sprite from File button and then drill down into the Things folder and select the button sprite and click on the window's OK button. Once the button sprite has been added, select it in the sprites list, click on the Costumes tab located at the top of the scripts area, and then click on the Edit button. This will open the sprite in the Paint Editor program. Click on the Text button located on the Paint Editor's toolbar and then specify ComicSans as the font type and 18 as the font size, type an uppercase letter A onto the middle of the button sprite, and then click on OK. Next, rename the sprite A.

Using the same series of steps outlined in the previous paragraph, add three additional instances of the button sprite to the application, naming them B, C, and D. Once added, align all four of the button sprites along the right-hand side of the stage, as demonstrated in Figures 7.13 and 7.14. At this point, you only have one last sprite to add. This sprite will need to be created from scratch. To do so, click on the Paint New Sprite button and then after specifying ComicSans as the font type and 18 as the font size, type **Welcome to the NBA trivia quiz!** as demonstrated in Figure 7.15 and click on the OK button.

Once added, reposition this new sprite at the top of the stage, as shown in Figures 7.13 and 7.14.

Step 4: Adding Variables Required by the Application

In order to execute, this application needs three variables as shown in Figure 7.16. To add these three variables to the application, click on the Variables button located at the top of the blocks palette and then click on the Make a Variable button three times to create three global variables named Answer, Clicked, and Score.

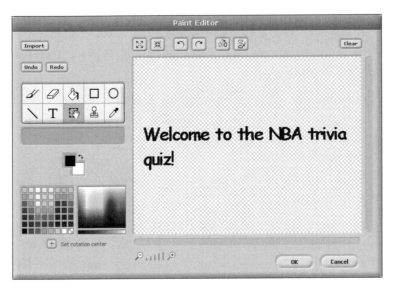

Figure 7.15
Creating a new sprite needed by the NBA Trivia Quiz.

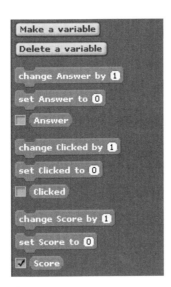

Figure 7.16
The NBA Trivia Quiz requires the addition of three global variables.

The variable named Answer will be used to keep track of the user's answers to each quiz question. The variable named Clicked will be used to control application execution, making sure that the script used to administer the quiz pauses and waits each time the user is prompted to answer a new question. The variable named Score will be used to keep track of the user's score (grade).

By default, Scratch will display monitors on the stage for all three of these variables. However, the game only needs to display the Score monitor. Therefore, you should clear the monitor check boxes for the Answer and Clicked variables. Also, the monitor for the Score variable needs to be moved to the lower right-hand corner of the stage.

Step 5: Adding Scripts to Button Sprites to Collect User Input

The programming logic that controls the overall administration of the quiz will be added to the host sprite, which is responsible for displaying quiz questions, collecting user answers, and then grading the results. In order to answer quiz questions, the user must click on one of the four sprite button (A, B, C, or D) when prompted by the hostess. Each of these four sprites has a small script belonging to it, which sets two variables when it is clicked. Below is the script that is executed when the A sprite is clicked.

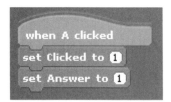

As you can see, this script begins with a hat block that executes whenever the A button is clicked. When this happens, the valued assigned to the Clicked variable is set to 1, and the value assigned to the Answer variable is also set to 1.

The Clicked variable is used in the application to keep track of when the user answers a question. This variable's value is set to 1 when the A sprite is clicked, indicating that the user has submitted an answer. Once the answer has been evaluated by a script belonging to the host sprite, the value of Clicked is set back to 0, making the application ready to process a new question. The Answer variable is used to identify which button has been clicked. Assigning a value of 1 to this variable indicates that the A sprite has been clicked.

The programming needed by the B sprite is shown next. As you can see, it is almost identical to the code assigned to the A sprite, with the value assigned to the Clicked variable being set to 1 when the button is clicked. Note that the value assigned to the Answer variable is 2, indicating that the second button (the B sprite) has been clicked.

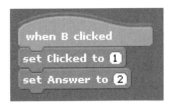

The code blocks that make up the C sprite scripts are shown next. As you can see, the third code block is used to identify when it is clicked.

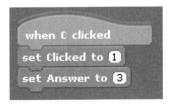

As you have probably anticipated, the code blocks that make up the script for the D sprite, shown next, assign a value of 4 to the Answer variable.

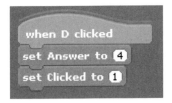

Step 6: Automating the Administration of the Quiz

At this point, you should have added scripts to each of the button sprites that indicate when they have been clicked and uniquely identify which of the four buttons was selected. Now it is time to create the two scripts belonging to the host sprite. The first script, shown next, is responsible for starting the application and getting the application ready to administer the quiz.

```
when [flag] clicked
set Score to (0)
set Clicked to (0)
set Answer to (0)
say [Welcome to the NBA tirivia quiz!] for (2) secs
say [Click on me when you are ready to begin.] for (2) secs
```

As you can see, this script has been set up to execute when the user clicks on the green flag button. When this happens, the values assigned to all three of the script's variables are set to 0 (setting the score to zero, indicating that none of the buttons have been clicked, and that no answer has been specified). Next, two looks code block are used to display instructions, welcoming the user and then instructing her to click on the hostess when ready to begin taking the quiz.

```
when Host clicked
wait (1) secs
say [On which NBA team did Michael Jordan play? A: Bulls,          B: Rockets, C: Celtics, D: Mavericks]
wait until < Clicked = (1) >
set Clicked to (0)
if < Answer = (1) >
    change Score by (20)
    say [Correct!] for (2) secs
else
    say [Incorrect!] for (2) secs
wait (1) secs
say [How many minutes make up a quarter? A: 8,  B: 10,  C: 12,    D: 15]
wait until < Clicked = (1) >
set Clicked to (0)
if < Answer = (3) >
    change Score by (20)
    say [Correct!] for (2) secs
else
    say [Incorrect!] for (2) secs
wait (1) secs
say [In which host city do the wizards play?    A: Washington,        B: Philadelphia,        C: Atlanta, D: Boston]
wait until < Clicked = (1) >
set Clicked to (0)
if < Answer = (1) >
    change Score by (20)
    say [Correct!] for (2) secs
else
    say [Incorrect!] for (2) secs
wait (1) secs
```

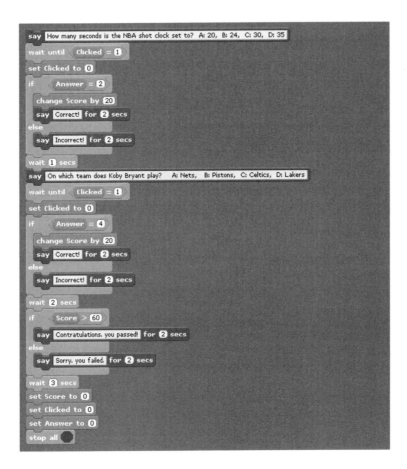

The host sprite's second script, shown here, is responsible for the overall administration of the quiz. As you can see, it is pretty big and is made up of many different types of code blocks, some of which you have not learned about yet. As such, only a high-level overview of the script will be provided in this chapter. Once you have read Chapters 9 and 10, you may want to return and review this script again.

This script begins with a hat code block that executes when the user clicks on the host sprite. Next, the script's execution is paused for one second, and then a looks block is used to display a text message, presenting the user with the quiz's first question. The next code block, which contains a pair of embedded code blocks, pauses script execution and waits until the value assigned to the Clicked variable is set to 1 (which will occur only when the user specifies an answer by clicking on one of the four button sprites).

The value assigned to Clicked is then reset to 0, making the variable ready for the next quiz question. Next, a control code block is used to evaluate the user's answer to the quiz question. This is accomplished by checking to see if the player clicked on the A sprite, as indicated by a value of 1 being assigned to Clicked. If this is the case, the user's score is increased by 20, and a looks block is used to display a text message informing the user that her answer was correct. If this is not the case, the user is notified that the answer provided was incorrect.

The next four quiz questions are administered using programming logic that is identical to that used to administer the first question, the only difference being that a different question is presented, and a different answer is required. Finally, once the last quiz question has been processed, the script's execution is paused for two seconds, after which the user's grade (the value assigned to Score) is evaluated to see if it is greater than 60, in which case the hostess announces that the user has passed the quiz. If this is not the case, the hostess announces that the user has failed. Either way, a three-second pause ensues, after which the values assigned to all three variables are reset to their default starting value of 0, to make the quiz ready for the next person. Finally, one last control block is executed, ensuring that all scripts within the application terminate their execution.

Step 7: Saving and Executing Your New Application

At this point, you have all the information needed to create your own copy of the NBA Trivia Quiz. Assuming that you have been following along and creating your copy of the application as you made your way through this chapter, then your application project should look something like the example shown in Figure 7.17.

If you have not done so, go ahead and save your new application. Once saved, switch to Presentation mode and start the NBA Trivia Quiz. As you test your new application, make sure that the feedback being provided by the hostess after each answer is correct. In addition, keep an eye on the Score monitor and make sure that the game is correctly tabulating your grade.

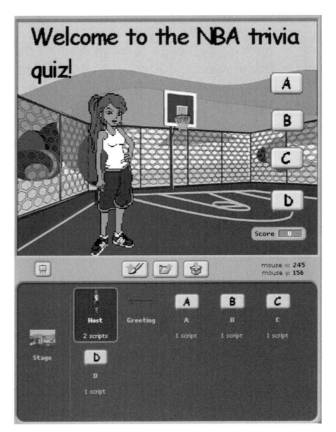

Figure 7.17
The completed application consists of a stage background, six sprites, and six scripts.

Summary

In this chapter you learned how to create variables and use them to store and retrieve numeric data. This included learning how to create both local and global variables and how to use them within Scratch projects to control the application execution. You also learned how to set up and configure variable monitors and to change variable values using a slider control. This chapter also showed you how to delete variables when you no longer need them.

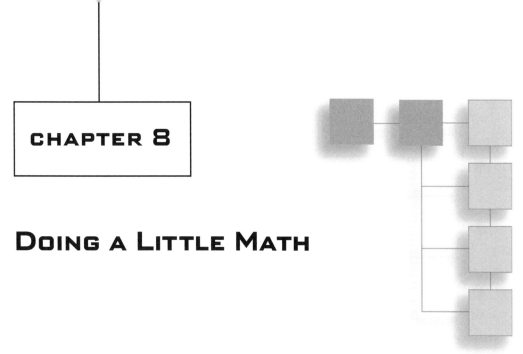

CHAPTER 8

DOING A LITTLE MATH

Scratch provides robust support for performing mathematical calculations. This gives you the ability to develop applications that can manipulate numeric data in a variety of ways. Scratch provides this support through numbers code blocks. Numbers code blocks are reporter blocks and therefore can only be used in conjunction with stack code blocks. This chapter will provide a thorough review of each of these code blocks and will also show you how to create a new Scratch application, the Number Guessing game.

The major topics covered in this chapter include:

- Learning how to add, subtract, multiply, and divide programmatically

- Learning how to generate random numbers using any range you specify

- Instruction on how to perform different types of numeric comparisons

- Learning how to perform a number of built-in mathematical operations

Addition, Subtraction, Multiplication, and Division

Like all modern programming languages, Scratch provides programmers with the ability to add, subtract, multiply, and divide numeric data. This capability is offered through the code blocks shown in Figure 8.1.

Figure 8.1
These code blocks provide Scratch programmers with the ability to perform arithmetic calculations.

The use of these code blocks is quite intuitive, with each code block clearly identifying its usage. These code blocks can be embedded within any Scratch code block that accepts numeric input. For example, the following script demonstrates how to use these code blocks to modify the value assigned to a variable named Count.

Here, the script begins by assigning an initial value of 10 to Count. Next, four sets of code blocks are executed. Each set consists of one stack block and two reporter blocks. The first set of statements sets the value of Count equal to the value currently assigned to Count plus 5, making Count equal to 15. The second set of code blocks sets Count equal to the value currently assigned to Count minus 5, making Count equal to 10. The third set of code blocks sets Count equal to the current value of Count times 5, making Count equal to 50. Lastly, the last set of code blocks changes the value of Count to 10 by dividing its current value by 5.

Understanding the Mathematical Order of Precedence

As is the case with all programming languages, Scratch allows you to string together different combinations of numbers code blocks in order to create more complicated numeric calculations. For example, take a look at the following script.

Here, a small script has been created that evaluates a numeric expression and assigns the result to a variable named Total. This equation was created by embedding a series of numbers code blocks within one another. Specifically, the

Figure 8.2
Creating complex formulas by assembling different combinations of code blocks.

equation was created by embedding the code blocks shown in Figure 8.2 into one another.

As shown in Figure 8.2, the equation was assembled by embedding the division code block into a variable block. Next, the addition code block was embedded within the left-hand side of the division code block. Finally, a multiplication code block and a subtraction code block are embedded within the input fields of the addition code block.

Like all programming languages, Scratch evaluates the components of mathematical expressions by following a specific order, referred to as the *order of precedence*. Specifically, Scratch evaluates an expression using a top-down approach. When applied to the example shown in Figures 8.2, Scratch evaluates it as follows:

1. First, it calculates the value of the two top code blocks. Therefore, 4 is multiplied by 5, yielding a value of 20, and 2 is subtracted from 4, yielding a value of 2. At this stage, the expression has been evaluated as shown here.

   `20 + 2 / 2`

2. Next, the expression located in the second level code bock (the addition block) is evaluated. Therefore, 20 is added to 2, yielding a value of 22. At this stage, the expression has been evaluated as shown here.

   `22 / 2`

3. Finally, the lowest level code block is evaluated, dividing 22 by 2 and resulting in a final value of 11.

Generating a Random Number

Some applications, such as computer games, require an element of randomness or chance. For example, a game that needs to simulate the rolling of dice needs to be able to create a pair of random numbers in the range of 1 to 6. Scratch provides the capability through the code block shown in Figure 8.3.

Figure 8.3
By default, this code block is configured to generate a number in the range of 1 to 10.

This code block provides a means of generating random integer (whole) numbers using any specified range of numbers. The default range is 1 to 10, but you may change the input fields to suit your needs. If needed, you can generate negative numbers. In addition to hard coding a numeric range into the control, you can substitute variable blocks by dragging and dropping them into either or both of this code block's input fields.

To develop an understanding of how this code block works, look at the following example:

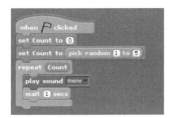

Here, a script has been created that begins by assigning a variable named Count a starting value of 0. Next, the variable's value is changed by assigning it a randomly selected value in the range of 1 to 5. A loop is then set up to repeat the execution of two embedded code blocks. The loop is designed to repeat a specified number of times and is set up by default to execute 10 times. However, by dragging and dropping an instance of the Count variable block into the loop's input field, the number of times that the loop executes is randomly determined, depending on the randomly assigned value of Count.

N o t e

Each time the loop executes, it plays an audio file that sounds like a cat meowing. In order to give the audio file time to finish playing, a control block was added to pause script execution for one second. To see this script in action, create a new Scratch application and add the script to the default Cat sprite.

Comparison Operations

In order to work with numbers, you often need to mathematically manipulate them as demonstrated in the previous section. Doing so will ultimately leave you with a result. Typically, you will want to do something with this result once it has

Figure 8.4
These code blocks provide the ability to compare any two numeric values.

been calculated. For a simple application, all you may need to do is display its value. However, more often than not, you are going to end up using it to guide the execution of your application in some manner. For example, suppose you want to create a number guessing game that automatically generates a random number and then challenges the player to try to guess it. Once the random number is generated and stored in a variable, the player needs to be prompted to. try to guess it (perhaps by clicking on one of 10 buttons with numbers printed on them). Once the player's guess is captured, the application needs to compare the player's guess against the value of the variable that stores the game's random number to determine whether the player's guess is correct. To facilitate this type of comparison operation, Scratch provides access to the three code blocks shown in Figure 8.4.

The first and last code blocks shown in Figure 8.4 allow you to compare one value against a range of values. The first code block checks to see if the numeric value specified in its first input field is less than the value specified in its second input field. The third code block does the opposite, checking to see if the numeric value specified in its first input field is greater than the value specified in its second input field. The middle code block is used to determine if two values are equal.

To develop a better understanding of how to work with each of these three code blocks, let's look at a few examples. In the first example, shown below, a script has been created that executes whenever the green flag button is clicked. When this happens, the value Count is set equal to 10. Next, a numbers block is embedded within a control block to set up a conditional test that evaluates the value assigned to Count and to execute the code block embedded within the control block in the event that the tested condition (Count equals 10) is true. Since this is the case, a text string of Hello! is displayed in a speech bubble.

Note

To prove that the embedded numbers code block is working as it is supposed to, you could change the value assigned to Count to something other than 10 and run the example again. Since the value assigned to Count no longer equals 10, the tested condition would evaluate as false, and the text message would not display.

In this next example, the numbers code block that tests for greater than conditions is used. Again, a script has been set up to execute whenever the green flag button is clicked. The value assigned to Count is then set to 1, and a control block is used to set up a loop that runs forever (until you provide a means for stopping its execution). A number of code blocks are embedded within the loop. The first block plays an audio file, and the second block pauses script execution for one second to allow Scratch time to finish playing the file. Another control block is then used to set up a conditional test that evaluates the value assigned to Count to see if it is greater than 2, and if it is, another control block is used to terminate the script's execution. If the value assigned to Count is not greater than 2, then the last code block located at the bottom of the loop is executed, incrementing the value of Count by 1. The loop then repeats and executes again.

The first time the loop runs, the value assigned to Count is 1. The loop must iterate two times before the value of Count is set to 3, resulting in the termination of the script's execution. Because of this, the audio file will play three times.

In this final example, shown next, the numbers code block that tests for less than conditions is used. Like the last two examples, this script is set up to execute whenever the green flag button is clicked. When this happens, the value of Count is set to 1. Next, a loop is set up that repeatedly executes as long as the value of Count is less than 15. Each time this test evaluates as true, three embedded code blocks are executed. The first code block moves the sprite 25 steps. The next code block increments the value assigned to Count by 1, and the last code block pauses script execution for one second.

The way this script is written, its loop will execute 14 times and will stop executing when the value of Count finally reaches 15.

Trick

While Scratch only supplies you with three code blocks for performing conditional tests (equality, greater than, and less than), most programming languages support three additional types of conditional tests, allowing you to perform the following comparison operations:

- Greater than or equal to

- Less than or equal to

- Not equal to

Although Scratch does not provide equivalent code blocks, you can easily set up equivalent comparison tests by combining the three code blocks just discussed with Scratch's logical comparison code blocks, as shown in Figure 8.5.

The first combination of code blocks shown in Figure 8.5 creates a test that determines if the value assigned to a variable named Total is less than or equal to 10. This example is made up of five code blocks—two variable blocks, two numbers code blocks used to perform less than and equality comparisons, and another numbers block, which is used to tie everything together. The second combination of code blocks shown in Figure 8.5 is very similar and is designed to create a test that checks to see if the value assigned to Total is greater than or equal to 5. The last example is made up of three code blocks and is used to evaluate the values assigned to Total to determine to see if it is not equal to 3. You will learn more about code blocks that support logical comparisons in the next section.

Figure 8.5
Creating customized logical comparisons.

Performing Logical Comparisons

In addition to code blocks designed to perform mathematical and comparison operations, Scratch also provides access to three code blocks that support logical comparison operations. These code blocks are shown in Figure 8.6.

The first code block is used to test two different sets of values to determine if both are true. The second code block is used to test two different sets of values to determine if at least one is true. And the last code block lets you evaluate two values to determine if the tested condition is false (not true).

To help you better understand how to work with all three of these code blocks, let's review a few examples. The first example, shown next, is a script that executes whenever the green flag button is clicked. When this occurs, the value assigned to the variable Count is set to 50. Next, a control code block is used to analyze the value assigned to Count. If the value of Count is less than 100 and also greater than 10, then the end statement embedded within the control block is executed. However, if both tested conditions evaluate as false, the embedded code block is not executed.

Note

Scratch is very flexible in its support for numbers blocks. For example, if you prefer, you could swap the order in which the two embedded numbers blocks occur (e.g., checking to see that Count is greater than 10 before checking to make sure that Count is also less than 100), and the results would be the same.

This next example is very similar to the previous example, except that instead of ensuring that both tested conditions evaluate as being true, the script has been

Figure 8.6
Using these code blocks, you can perform more complex comparison operations.

modified so that only one of the tested conditions has to be evaluated as true in order for the embedded code block to be executed.

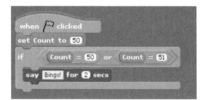

This final example shows a script that performs a negative test, checking to see if two values are not equal instead of checking to see if they are equal. As a result, if the value assigned to Count is not equal to 50, which it is not, the code block embedded within the control block is executed.

Rounding Numbers and Retrieving Remainders

The next set of numbers code blocks, shown in Figure 8.7, provides the ability to retrieve the remainder portion of any division operation and lets you round any decimal number to the nearest whole number.

The first code block shown in Figure 8.7 returns the remainder portion of a division operation, also referred to as a modulus, as demonstrated in the following example, which divides 10 by 3 and then assigns the modulus (a value of 1) to a variable named Remainder.

Figure 8.7
These code blocks retrieve remainders and round numbers.

The second code block shown in Figure 8.7 returns the rounded value for a specified numeric value, rounded to the nearest whole number, as demonstrated in the following examples, which return values of 4 and 5, respectively.

Working with Built-in Mathematical Functions

In addition to all of the mathematical operations that you can put together using the numbers code blocks previously discussed in this chapter, Scratch provides one additional multi purpose code block, as shown in Figure 8.8.

This code block is designed to perform any of 12 different mathematical functions, which can be selected from the code block's drop-down list. The functions that this code block can perform are outlined in the following list:

- **abs.** Returns the absolute, non-negative value of a number.

- **sqrt.** Returns the square root of a number.

- **sin.** Returns a value representing the sine of an angle.

- **cos.** Returns a value representing the cosine of an angle.

- **tan.** Returns a value representing the tangent of an angle.

- **asin.** Returns the arc sine for the specified numeric value.

- **acos.** Returns the arc cosine for the specified numeric value.

- **atan.** Returns the arc tangent for the specific numeric value.

- **ln.** Returns the inverse of the natural exponent of a specified value (i.e., the opposite of e^).

- **log.** Returns the natural log of a number.

Figure 8.8
This code block can assist you in setting up extremely complex calculations.

- **e^.** Returns the natural exponent of a specified value.

- **10^.** Returns the value of a number raised to the 10th power.

These code blocks can be real time savers when developing applications that require the use of any of the mathematical functions supported by the code block, saving you the trouble of implementing the underlying programming logic yourself to retrieve similar results. As a result, not only will you spend less time working on the development of your application, but the programming logic that you have to develop will be simplified and easier to maintain, since this code block can do most of the heavy lifting for you.

To specify which function you want to work with, all you have to do is select it from the code block's drop-down list. For example, the following examples demonstrate the use of two different functions provided by this code block:

This example consists of two sets of code blocks. The first set of code blocks returns the absolute value of −4.4, which is 4.4, and assigns that value to a variable named `Result`. The second set of blocks returns the square root of 9, which is 3, and assigns that value to a variable named `Result`.

Developing the Number Guessing Game Quiz Project

The remainder of this chapter is focused on the development of your next Scratch application, the Number Guessing game. This application will make use of numbers code blocks to generate random numbers for the player to guess and to compare the player's guesses against the game's randomly generated number.

In total, the application is made up of a background, 11 sprites, and 12 scripts. When run, the game will challenge the player to guess a randomly generated number in the range of 0 to 9 in as few guesses as possible. Figure 8.9 shows an example of how the game looks when first started.

To enter a guess, the player must click on one of the button sprites located at the bottom of the stage. The cat provides immediate feedback after each guess, as demonstrated in Figure 8.10.

Figure 8.9
The Number Guessing game is moderated by the Cat sprite.

Figure 8.10
The cat lets the player know when guesses are too high or too low.

Figure 8.11
The player guessed the secret number in five guesses.

Figure 8.11 shows how the game looks once the player finally manages to guess the game's secret random number.

The game automatically generates a new random number at the end of each game, in order to ready the game to be played again. The development of this application project will be created by following a series of steps, as outlined here:

1. Creating a new Scratch application project.

2. Adding a background to the stage.

3. Adding and removing sprites.

4. Adding variables needed by the application.

5. Adding an audio file to the application.

6. Adding scripts to each button to collect player guesses.

7. Adding the programming logic required to process player guesses.

8. Saving and executing your work.

Step 1: Creating a New Scratch Project

The first step in the development of the Number Guessing game is to create a new Scratch application project. To do so, start Scratch, automatically creating a new Scratch project or, if Scratch is already running, click on the New button located on the Scratch menu bar.

Step 2: Adding a Stage Background

The next step in the development of the Number Guessing game is to add a background to the stage. To do so, click on the blank stage thumbnail located in the sprite list and then change its background by clicking on the Backgrounds tab located at the top of the scripts area. Next, click on the Import button and when the Import Background window opens, click on the Outdoors folder. Then select the `brick-wall1` thumbnail and click on the OK button. Since the application only needs one background, remove the default blank background, named `background1`, from your project by clicking on the Delete This Costume button.

Step 3: Adding and Removing Sprites

The Number Guessing game is comprised of the default `Cat` sprite plus 10 button sprites and a variable monitor, as shown in Figure 8.12.

Figure 8.12
An overview of the different parts of the Number Guessing game.

To add the first of the sprites representing the 10 input buttons, click on the Choose New Sprite from File button to open the New Sprite window. Drill down in to the Letters folder and then the Keys folder to select the 0 sprite. Then click on the OK button. Place the sprite in the lower-left corner of the stage, as shown in Figure 8.12. Following this same process, add sprites 1 through 9 to the bottom of the stage as well. At this point, all that is left in the design of the application's user interface is the display and repositioning of the monitor, which you will do in the next step.

Step 4: Adding Variables Required by the Application

In order to execute, the Number Guessing game requires three variables, as shown in Figure 8.13. To add these variables to the application, click on the

Figure 8.13
The Number Guessing game requires three variables.

Variables button located at the top of the blocks palette and then click on the Make a Variable button three times to define variables named Guess, No Of Guesses, and RandomNo.

The variable named Guess will be used to store the most recent guess made by the player. The variable named No Of Guesses will be used to keep track of the number of guesses made by the player during each game. The variable named RandomNo will be used to store the game's randomly generated secret number. Once added, clear the check box controls belonging to the Guess and No Of Guesses variables to prevent their monitors from being displayed. Lastly, drag and drop the monitor for the No Of Guesses variable to the middle right-hand side of the stage.

Step 5: Adding an Audio File to the Application

The Number Guessing game makes use of two audio files that are played as sound effects when the player makes incorrect and correct guesses. The audio file played when the player enters a missed guess is the default pop file, which is automatically included as part of each of the button sprites used in the application. The second audio file is the Fairydust file, which is played whenever the player manages to correctly guess the mystery number.

To add the Fairydust audio file, select the Cat sprite thumbnail in the sprite list and then click on the Sounds tab located at the top of the scripts area. Next, click on the Import button to display the Import Sound window, and then double-click on the Electronic folder, select the Fairydust file, and click on OK.

Step 6: Adding Scripts to Capture Player Input

The programming logic that drives the Number Guessing application is divided into a series of scripts belonging to the application's sprites. Specifically, small scripts must be added to each of the button sprites to capture and save player guesses. In addition, two scripts must be added to the Cat sprite. These two scripts, which are responsible for starting the game and processing player guesses, will be covered in Step 7.

To begin work on each of the scripts belonging to the button sprites, select the sprite representing the 0 button and then add the following code blocks to it:

The script begins with a hat block that executes whenever the sprite is clicked (when the player clicks on it as a guess). When this occurs, the second code block in the script sends a Player has guessed broadcast message to the other sprites as a signal that the player has submitted a guess. The Player has guessed must be typed into the control block exactly as shown. A third code block is then used to assign a value to the Guess variable, recording the player's guess. Note that in this example, setting Guess to 0 indicates that the player has submitted a guess of 0. The last code block in the script plays the default pop audio file, which lets the player know that the guess has been processed.

Note

A *broadcast message* is a message exchanged between sprites that signals when an event of some type has occurred within an application. Broadcast messages are generated by and received using various control code blocks, which you will learn all about in Chapter 10, "Changing the Way Sprites Look and Behave." For now, all you need to know is that this application uses broadcast messages in order to coordinate activity and keep track of what is occurring within the game.

The scripts that need to be added to the rest of the button sprites are almost identical to the script that you just added. The only difference is that you need to modify the value that is set in the third code block to properly reflect which button sprite each script belongs to. The easiest way to add these scripts to the other nine button sprites is to drag and drop an instance of the first script onto each of the nine other sprites and then to select each sprite, one at a time, and modify the value of the third code block accordingly.

Step 7: Processing Player Guesses

Once scripts have been added to all 10 of the button sprites, it is time to create the two scripts belonging to the Cat sprite. The first of these scripts is shown next and is responsible for initializing the game and getting it ready to play.

This script is executed when the player clicks on the green flag button. It begins by assigning an initial value of 0 to No Of Guesses and then assigns a randomly generated value in the range of 0 to 9 to a variable named RandomNo. Lastly, it displays a pair of messages that inform the player that the cat is thinking of a number and challenges the player to try to guess it.

The second and final script to be added to the Cat sprite is shown next. This script is automatically executed whenever the Player has guessed broadcast message is received. This happens when the player clicks on one of the 10 button sprites. First, the script modifies the value assigned to No Of Guesses by increasing it by 1. This allows the application to keep track of the number of guesses that the player has made in the current game.

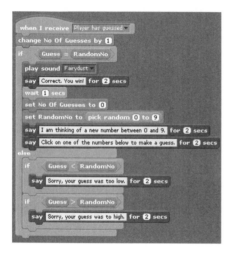

The rest of the script is made up of code blocks embedded within a control block. The control block begins by evaluating the value assigned to the Guess variable to see if it is equal to the value assigned to the RandomNo variable. If this is the case, a series of code blocks embedded within the upper portion of the control block are executed. If this is not the case, code blocks embedded in the bottom of the control block are executed.

The code statements located in the upper half of the control block, which execute when the player enters a correct guess, perform the following actions:

- Play the Fairydust audio file that was added to the Cat sprite back in Step 5
- Notify the player that the game has been won
- Pause script execution for one second
- Reset the value of No Of Guesses to 0

- Select a new random number for the game

- Challenge the player to play again

If, on the other hand, the player enters an incorrect guess, the code blocks embedded at the bottom of the script are executed. These code blocks are organized into two separate control blocks. The first control block evaluates the value assigned to Guess to see if it is less than RandomNo, and if it is, a message is displayed that informs the player that the guess was too low. The second control block determines if the value assigned to Guess is less than RandomNo, and if it is, a message is displayed that informs the player that the guess was too high.

Step 8: Saving and Executing Your New Scratch Application

At this point, you now have all the information that you need to create your own copy of the Number Guessing game. If you have not already done so, save your new Scratch project. Once saved, switch to Presentation mode, run the game, and put it through its paces. Remember to begin game play by clicking on the green flag button and following the instructions provided by the Cat sprite.

Summary

This chapter provided a thorough overview of Scratch numbers code blocks and demonstrated their usage. This included learning how to perform mathematical calculations and generate random numbers, as well as how to perform numeric comparisons. You learned how to perform different types of logical comparisons and to combine code blocks that execute logical and comparison operations to carry out advanced comparison operations. On top of all this, you learned how to perform a host of advanced mathematical operations like rounding numbers and executing different arithmetic functions. You also learned how to create another Scratch application, the Number Guessing game.

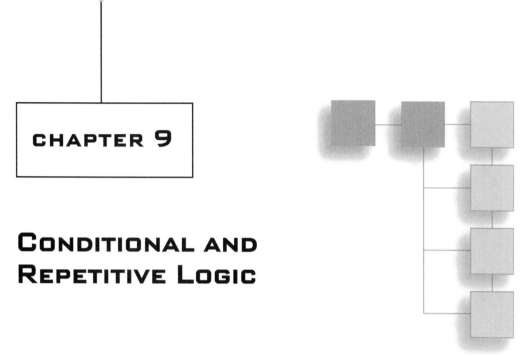

CHAPTER 9

CONDITIONAL AND REPETITIVE LOGIC

To create a script, you must know how to work with control code blocks. All of Scratch's hat blocks are control blocks. Control blocks also provide the capability to implement loops and conditional programming logic, which are the building blocks of advanced and complex applications. Control blocks can pause and halt script execution. Control blocks also provide the capability to send and receive broadcast messages, providing you with a means of coordinating application activity.

The major topics covered in this chapter include:

- How to use control blocks to initiate script execution

- How to pause and halt script execution

- How to set up different types of loops and implement conditional programming logic

- How to send and receive broadcast messages between sprites

Introducing Scratch Control Blocks

Scratch control blocks provide programmers with many different capabilities, all of which are geared around controlling script execution. Without control blocks, scripts would not be able to execute. Nor would they be able to pause, loop, or execute conditional logic when evaluating data. Through control blocks, Scratch can perform all of the actions listed here:

- Event programming

- Pause script execution

- Create loops

- Send and receive broadcast messages

- Execute conditional logic

- Halt script execution

You have already seen control blocks in action in every script presented in the first eight chapters of this book. Now it is time to learn more about these powerful code blocks and the programming features they provide.

Event Programming

Control blocks can initiate script execution, which is critical to the execution of Scratch applications. This is accomplished with hat blocks, including those shown in Figure 9.1.

As you have seen in many examples in this book, the first code block shown in Figure 9.1 initiates a script's execution whenever the green flag button is clicked, and it is the most common means of starting an application's execution. For example, if you were to add the following script to any sprite or background in a Scratch application, it would automatically play a specified audio file (provided that file has been imported).

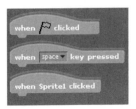

Figure 9.1
Hat blocks automate the execution of scripts.

The second code block shown in Figure 9.1 initiates a script's execution whenever a specified keyboard key is pressed. The key that is used as the trigger is selected by clicking on the code block's drop-down list and making a selection of one of the following keystrokes:

- Up, down, right, and left arrow keys

- The spacebar

- a – z

- 0 – 9

For example, the following script demonstrates how to move a sprite by 50 steps whenever the keyboard's spacebar is pressed:

The third code block shown in Figure 9.1 initiates script execution whenever the sprite to which it belongs is clicked. The following script demonstrates how to use this code block to automate the display of text in a speech bubble whenever the sprite to which it has been added is clicked:

Note

Scratch provides a fourth hat control block, which is covered later in this chapter. This code block is used to initiate script execution when broadcast messages are received.

Pausing Script Execution

Once started, scripts execute without pause until they are done. However, sometimes you need to temporarily pause a script's execution for a specified period. The code block that you need to use in this type of situation is shown in Figure 9.2.

Figure 9.2
Using this control block, you can pause script execution for as long as necessary.

This code block adds brief pauses to your Scratch applications. For example, you might want to pause a script's execution for a second or two after the player scores a point. This brief pause would allow the player a moment to review the score and to get ready for the next point. Another reason for pausing a script's execution is to help manage the playback of audio files, as demonstrated in the following example:

Here, you see a script that plays two audio files. In order to allow the first audio file time to play back, the script is paused for two seconds, after which execution resumes, and the second audio file is played. If you were to remove the control block that pauses the script from this example, both audio files would play simultaneously, interfering with one another.

Tip

It you want to continuously play an audio file without pausing a script's execution, consider putting the code statements that are responsible for audio file playback in their own script and adding that script to the stage.

Note

The control block shown in Figure 9.3 also pauses script execution, waiting until a specified condition becomes true. This code block is covered a little later in this chapter, when conditional programming logic is discussed.

Figure 9.3
This code block provides another way of conditionally pausing script execution.

Executing Loops

Most computer applications and games are interactive, meaning that they respond to user input and react accordingly. In doing so, it is often necessary to execute collections of code statements repeatedly. For example, an arcade-style computer game might require the continuous playback of background music and sound effects. This would require the repeated execution of programming logic required to manage sound playback for as long as the game was played. To manage this type of interaction, you need to add loops to your applications. In Scratch, a *loop* is a collection of one or more code blocks embedded with a control block that are repeatedly executed.

Without loops, programmers would have to create extremely large scripts filled with repeated series of duplicate statements to perform certain tasks. For example, to create a Scratch application that bounces the Cat sprite up and down four times without a loop, would you have to add a script like the one shown next to the sprite.

```
when [flag] clicked
go to x: 0 y: -130
glide 0.5 secs to x: 0 y: 0
glide 0.5 secs to x: 0 y: -130
glide 0.5 secs to x: 0 y: 0
glide 0.5 secs to x: 0 y: -130
glide 0.5 secs to x: 0 y: 0
glide 0.5 secs to x: 0 y: -130
glide 0.5 secs to x: 0 y: 0
glide 0.5 secs to x: 0 y: -130
```

The script begins by positioning the sprite at the bottom center of the stage. Two sets of motion blocks are needed to bounce the sprite one time. So to bounce the sprite up and down four times, these two code block have to be repeated four times. Suppose you wanted to make the sprite bounce 10, 100, or 1,000 times. Clearly, this is a situation where a loop is needed.

Scratch supplies access to two code blocks that you can use to set up loops, as shown in Figure 9.4.

Note

Scratch also supplies two additional control blocks that offer the capability to conditionally execute loops. These two code blocks will be discussed a little later in this chapter when conditional logic is covered.

Figure 9.4
Using these code blocks, you can create loops that repeat the execution of any code blocks you embedded within them.

The first of the two code blocks shown in Figure 9.4 can be set up as a loop that executes forever, which really means that the loop repeatedly executes until the script in which it resides is halted. For example, the following script uses this code block to set up a loop that bounces a sprite over and over again, until the Stop Everything button is clicked:

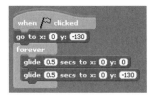

The first statement moves the sprite to the bottom center of the stage. The two statements within the loop bounce the sprite, in a gliding motion, up and down from the bottom to the middle of the stage.

Note

In Scratch, there are two ways to force an immediate termination of a script. First, you can halt a script by stopping the execution of the application by clicking on the red Stop Everything button. However, this option can often be a bit of overkill. As a less extreme option, Scratch offers a control block that allows you to halt an individual script's execution. There is also a control block that you can use to halt the execution of all scripts within an application. Both of these control blocks are reviewed a little later in this chapter.

Rather than repeating the execution of a loop forever, you can use the second code block shown in Figure 9.4 to set up a loop that executes a predetermined number of times. For example, the following script demonstrates how to bounce a sprite up and down a total of 10 times.

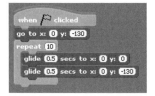

Obviously, the fewer code blocks you use when developing scripts, the more streamlined and easier to support your applications will be. Loops make programming a lot easier and provide a tool that you can use to repeat the execution of any number of code statements with as little fuss as possible.

Sending and Receiving Broadcasts

Because Scratch applications can be made up of many different sprites, each of which may consist of many different scripts, coordinating the activity of all the different parts of the application can be challenging. By providing access to the three code blocks shown in Figure 9.5, Scratch offers the ability to send and receive broadcast messages as a means of coordinating script execution.

Using the first two code blocks shown in Figure 9.5, you can pass messages to any script within an application that begins with the hat code block shown at the bottom of Figure 9.5. For example, the following script demonstrates how to send a broadcast message of jump to all sprites within the application:

To specify the message sent by the control code block, all you have to do is click on the block's drop-down list and then either select a previously typed message or create a new message by clicking on New and then typing in the message. This particular code block sends its message and then allows the script in which it is embedded to continue executing. Alternatively, the following script not only sends a broadcast message but also waits until every script in the application, which has been set up to execute when the message is sent, has finished executing:

Using the hat block, you can set up a script to execute whenever a specified message is received.

Figure 9.5
Broadcast messages provide the capability for one script to notify other scripts that an event has occurred.

Note

Using the three previous scripts, you could create a new application made up of two button controls and the default Cat sprite. By assigning the first script to the first button sprite, the second script to the second button sprite, and the third script to the Cat sprite, you can make the Cat sprite jump up and down on the stage any time you click on one of the button sprites.

Conditional Programming Logic

The next set of control code blocks provided by Scratch is shown in Figure 9.6. These code blocks allow you to apply conditional programming logic to your scripts.

Using these code blocks, you can analyze data within your applications and make decisions based on this analysis, resulting in the conditional execution of collections of code blocks. The key concept to understand when working with these types of code blocks is that conditional logic involves an evaluation as to whether a condition is true or not. If the condition being analyzed is true, then the code blocks embedded within the control block are executed. However, if the condition being analyzed proves false, the embedded code blocks are not executed.

The following script demonstrates how to use the first code block shown in Figure 9.6 to set up a loop in which execution is controlled by a conditional test. Each time the loop repeats, it checks the value assigned to a variable named Counter to see if it is equal to 0. If it is, the loop executes, plays an audio file, pauses for two seconds, and then checks to see if it should execute again.

Figure 9.6
These five code blocks let you conditionally execute collections of code blocks.

This next example demonstrates how to conditionally execute the playback of an audio file. When executed, this script examines the value assigned to a variable named Counter to see if it is equal to 0, and if it is, the audio file is played.

Sometimes you may want to execute either of two sets of code blocks based on the results of a tested condition. This can be accomplished using the third code block shown in Figure 9.6.

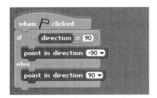

Here, a conditional test is performed that checks to see if the direction that a sprite is facing is 90 degrees. If it is, the direction that the sprite is pointing is reversed. If you run the script repeatedly, the direction that the sprite is pointing is continuously reversed.

This next example demonstrates how to use a control block that pauses script execution and waits for a specified condition to become true.

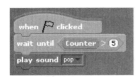

Here, a script has been set up that, once run, checks on the value assigned to Counter to see if it is greater than 5. If it is, an audio file is played. If Counter is not greater than 5, then the script pauses its execution, waiting until the value of Counter exceeds 5 before finishing its execution.

Finally, the last example demonstrates how to work with the last of the control blocks shown in Figure 9.6. Here, a loop is set up to execute repeatedly until the value assigned to Counter is set equal to 3, at which time the loops will stop running. Each time the loop runs, it moves, or bounces, its associated sprite up and down on the stage.

Nesting Conditional Control Code Blocks

As powerful as the control blocks are that facilitate conditional execution, they are limited to analyzing a single condition at a time. To develop more complex programming logic, you can embed one control block within another, as demonstrated in the following example:

Here, one control block has been embedded within another control block to further analyze the value assigned to Counter. If necessary, you can embed control blocks many levels deep. However, the deeper you go, the more difficult your scripts will be to understand and maintain.

Preventing Endless Loops

Loops are extremely powerful tools, providing the capability to perform repetitive tasks with ease. However, if you are not careful when setting them up, you can accidentally set up an endless loop. An *endless loop* is a loop that, because of a logical error on the programmer's part, never ends. For example, you might want to set up a loop that plays an audio file five times. But suppose when setting up the loop you made a mistake that prevented the loop from ever terminating, as shown here.

Here, the intention was to set up a loop that would execute five times. The loop has been set up to execute for as long as the value assigned to Counter is less than 5. Counter is assigned an initial value of 1, and its value is supposed to be incremented by 1 each time the loop executes. However, instead of incrementing the value of Counter by 1 at the end of the loop, the value of Counter is decremented by a value of -1. As a result, the loop never terminates, forever repeating the playback of the audio file. To prevent endless loops from occurring, you need to take extra care when setting up loops and test your scripts thoroughly when developing your applications.

Terminating Script Execution

The last two control blocks offered by Scratch are shown in Figure 9.7. These code blocks programmatically halt script execution within your Scratch applications.

Using the first of these two control blocks, you can halt the execution of the scripts in which the code block is placed, as demonstrated in the following example:

Here, the script checks to see if the value assigned to a variable named Counter is equal to 3, and if it is, an audio file is played. If Counter is not equal to 3, then a different audio file is played, and the script's execution is halted. Halting a script this way forces its immediate termination, even if the script contains additional code blocks that have not been executed.

Using the second control block shown in Figure 9.7, you can not only halt the execution of the current script, but you can also halt the execution of every script in the application. For example, the following script executes a loop three times and then halts the execution of every script in the application in which it resides.

Figure 9.7
Using these code blocks, you can halt the execution of any or all scripts within an application.

Developing the Ball Chase Game

The rest of this chapter is dedicated to teaching you how to create your next Scratch application, the Ball Chase game. This application makes heavy use of different control blocks to control the movement of the ball and the cat that chases it around the stage. In total, the application is made up of four sprites and nine scripts. The object of the game is to try to prevent the cat from catching the ball as it chases it around the stage. If you can keep the ball out of the cat's reach for 30 seconds, you win. Figure 9.8 shows how the game looks when first started.

To play, all you have to do is move the mouse-pointer around the stage, and the ball will automatically follow. If the cat manages to catch the ball before 30 seconds is up, the game ends, as demonstrated in Figure 9.9.

Figure 9.8
The object of the game is to prevent the cat from catching the ball.

Figure 9.9
The game ends if the cat catches the ball.

Figure 9.10
The player wins if the ball can be kept away from the cat for 30 seconds.

Figure 9.10 shows how the game looks when the player successfully manages to evade the cat for the entire 30 seconds.

The development of this application will be accomplished by following a series of steps, as outlined here:

1. Creating a new Scratch project.

2. Adding and removing sprites.

3. Adding variables needed by the application.

4. Adding an audio file to the application.

5. Adding a script to control ball movement.

6. Adding scripts that display game over messages.

7. Adding the scripts required to control and coordinate game play.

8. Saving and executing your work.

Step 1: Creating a New Scratch Project

The first step in the development of the Ball Chase game is to create a new Scratch project. To do so, start Scratch, automatically creating a new Scratch project, or if Scratch is already running, click on the New button located on the Scratch menu bar.

Step 2: Adding and Removing Sprites

The Ball Chase game is made up of the default Cat sprite plus three other sprites and a variable monitor, as shown in Figure 9.11.

Figure 9.11
An overview of the different parts of the Ball Chase game.

Since the default Cat sprite is not needed in this application, go ahead and remove it. In its place you need to add a different sprite, representing a top-down view of a different Cat sprite. To add this sprite, click on the Choose New Sprite from File button. When the New Sprite window opens, drill down in to the Animals folder and then select the cat2 sprite and click on the OK button. By default, the sprite is placed in the middle of the stage and faces in a 90-degree direction. Leave this sprite in its default location in the middle of the stage, change its direction to 0, and then change its assigned name to Cat. Next, add the Ball sprite by clicking on the Choose New Sprite from File button, drilling down in to the Things folder, selecting the beachball1 sprite, and then clicking on the OK button. Place the Ball sprite on the top center of the stage and change its assigned named to Ball.

To add the application's remaining two sprites, which will be nothing more than text strings saved as sprites, you must create them, which you can do using Scratch's built-in Paint Editor program. Both of these sprites consist of text messages. For the first of these two sprites, open the Paint Editor by clicking on the Paint New Sprite button. When the Paint Editor program opens, specify a font type of ComicSans, a font color of red, and a font size of 18. Type **Game Over,** press the Enter key, type **You lose!** into the Paint Editor, and then click on the OK button. Using this same process, create a second sprite that says **Game Over! You win.** Change the names assigned to these two sprites to LosingMsg and WinningMsg, respectively.

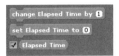

Figure 9.12
The Ball Chase game requires one variable.

Step 3: Adding Variables Required by the Application

To execute, the Ball Chase game requires one variable as shown in Figure 9.12. To add this variable to the application, click on the Variables button located at the top of the blocks palette and then click on the Make a Variable button to define a variable named Elapsed Time.

This variable will be used to display the amount of time remaining in the game. Make sure that you leave the check box for this variable selected and that you reposition the variable's corresponding monitor to the upper right-hand corner of the stage.

Step 4: Adding an Audio File to the Application

The Ball Chase game makes use of one sound effect, which simulates the meowing of the cat as its chases the ball around the stage. To add this audio file, select the Cat sprite thumbnail in the sprite list and then click on the Sounds tab located at the top of the scripts area. Next, click on the Import button to display the Import Sound window, double-click on the Animal folder, select the Meow audio file, and finally click on the OK button to finish adding the audio file to the sprite.

Step 5: Adding a Script to Control Ball Movement

The objective of the game is to try to keep the ball out of the reach of the cat for 30 seconds. The following script, which should be added to the Ball sprite, is responsible for controlling the movement of the ball on the stage.

This script begins with a hat block. Next, a motion block is used to position the ball in the upper middle portion of the stage. A looks block is then used to move the sprite back one layer, ensuring that if the Ball sprite encounters the Cat sprite, the Ball sprite will be displayed under the Cat sprite instead of on top of it. (You will learn about looks blocks in Chapter 10, "Changing the Way Sprites Look and Behave.")

The rest of the script consists of a loop that repeatedly executes another motion block. The motion block is responsible for moving the Ball sprite around the stage to where the mouse-pointer is.

Step 6: Adding Scripts That Display Game Over Messages

You will add the script that is responsible for making the cat chase the ball around the stage in the next section. Before doing so, add the following pair of scripts to the WinningMsg sprite. These scripts are responsible for displaying and hiding the game's winning message.

The first of the two scripts shown above is responsible for hiding the display of the sprite to which it has been added. The second script, on the other hand, is responsible for displaying the sprite whenever a broadcast message of You win is received. Note that this script includes a looks block that pushes the sprite to the front of any other sprites that it may happen to overlap. This ensures that the message is completely visible once displayed.

Once you have created and added these two scripts to the WinningMsg sprite, drag and drop both of them onto the LosingMsg sprite and then edit the second script so that it executes whenever a broadcast message of You lose is received.

Step 7: Adding Scripts Needed to Control and Coordinate Game Play

To wrap up your work on the Ball Chase game, you need to add four scripts to the Cat sprite. The first of these scripts is shown next and is responsible for ensuring the cat chases the ball around the stage.

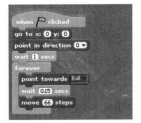

This script begins by moving the Cat sprite to the center of the stage and pointing it in its default upward direction. Next, it pauses for one second and then enters into a loop, which repeatedly executes the embedded code blocks. The first of these three code blocks points the cat sprite towards the Ball sprite. The second code block pauses the loop's execution for .15 seconds, after which the third block moves the Cat sprite 66 steps in the direction of the Ball sprite.

Note

The reason for imposing the .15 second delay in the script's loop is to slow down things enough to give the player a chance to keep the ball from the cat. If the little extra delay were removed from the loop, the speed at which the cat moves would easily overcome even the fastest player.

The second of the four scripts to be added to the Cat sprite is shown next. This script is set to execute when the player starts the game by clicking on the green flag button. The script begins by setting the value at which the audio is played to 50% of the level of the computer's current sound level. The rest of the script is controlled by a loop that repeatedly runs two embedded code blocks. The first code block pauses script execution for five seconds. The second code block plays the Meow audio file. The result is that the cat will meow every five seconds as it chases the ball around the stage.

The third script to be added to the Cat sprite is responsible for halting the execution of all scripts in the application in the event that the cat manages to touch the sprite during game play. The code blocks that make up this script are shown here:

This script is executed when the player starts the game by clicking on the green flag button. The script's overall execution is controlled by a loop. Within the loop, a conditional test is performed that checks to see if the Cat sprite has made contact with the Ball sprite. If this is the case, a broadcast message of You lose is sent. Once this message has been received and processed by the other scripts in the application, the last code block in the loop is executed, halting all script execution.

The last script to be added to the Cat sprite is shown next. This script is responsible for keeping track of time as the application executes and for halting game play after 30 seconds, should the player manage to keep the cat at bay for that long.

When started, this script begins by resetting Scratch's internal timer and then assigning the current value of the timer (0.0) to a variable named Elapsed Time. The rest of the script is controlled by a loop. Each time the loop executes, it updates the value assigned to the Elapsed Time variable to reflect the timer's current value. Next, a check is made to see if the timer's value has exceeded 30 seconds, and if it has, a broadcast message of You win is sent. Once processed by the other scripts in the application, the execution of all scripts in the application is halted. If, on the other hand, the timer's value is less than 30 seconds, the loop simply executes again. Accordingly, if the cat does not manage to catch the ball within 30 seconds, thus ending the game, the fourth script will end the game and declare the player to be the winner.

Step 8: Saving and Executing Your Scratch Project

All right! Assuming you have followed along closely with each of the steps presented in this chapter, your copy of the Ball Chase game should be ready for testing. If you have not done so yet, save your new Scratch project. Once saved, switch over to Presentation mode and execute the game. Remember that game play begins when you click on the green flag button and that your object is to keep the ball out of the cat's reach for 30 seconds.

Summary

This chapter provided an overview of all of Scratch's control blocks. You learned how to use Scratch hat blocks and to pause and halt script execution. This chapter also showed you how to set up different types of loops and to work with all five of Scratch's control blocks that support conditional programming logic. You also learned how to control and coordinate script activity by sending and receiving broadcast messages between sprites.

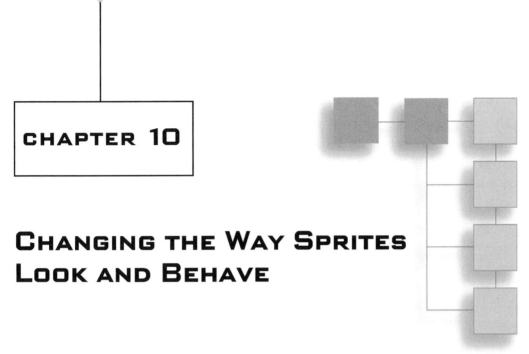

CHAPTER 10

CHANGING THE WAY SPRITES LOOK AND BEHAVE

By its very nature, Scratch lends itself to the development of graphical applications that involve the manipulation of sprites. This includes taking actions that affect the appearance and behavior of both sprites and the stage background. Sprite and background appearance and behavior can be controlled using looks code blocks. Looks code blocks can be used to affect sprite appearance through the application of special effects, to make sprites visible or invisible as applications execute, and even to change sprite costumes and stage backgrounds. This chapter offers an in-depth overview of all of Scratch's looks code blocks and will guide you through the creation of your next Scratch project, the Crazy Eight Ball game.

The major topics covered in this chapter include:

- Learning how to programmatically change a sprite's costume

- Learning how to display text in speech and thought bubbles

- Discovering how to apply a range of special graphical effects to sprites

- Learning how to change a sprite's size

- Making sprites appear and disappear during application execution

- Specifying how sprites that overlap one another should be displayed

Changing Sprite Costumes and Backgrounds

Depending on whether you have selected a sprite's thumbnail or the stage thumbnail in the sprite list, several different code blocks are displayed when you look at Scratch's looks blocks in the blocks palette. For starters, the first three code blocks are different, as shown in Figure 10.1.

Both sets of code blocks have similar tasks, with one set focusing on working with sprite costumes while the other set is focused on working with the stage's background.

Changing Sprite Costumes

Every sprite that is added to a Scratch application is capable of changing its appearance by changing its costume. Sprites can be assigned any number of costumes and switch between them at any time. To add a costume to a sprite, all you have to do is select the sprite's thumbnail, click on the Costumes tab located at the top of the scripts area, and then click on the Import button. This opens a window that allows you to locate and select a graphic file to be used as a new costume for the sprite.

Every costume that is added to a sprite is automatically assigned a number and a name (based on the graphic's filename). The first costume in the costume list represents the sprite when the application is started. However, using drag and drop, you can rearrange the order in which costumes are listed. In addition, using the first looks block shown in Figure 10.1, you can programmatically replace a sprite's current costume by specifying the name of a different costume. For example, the following script demonstrates how to use this code block in a loop to repeatedly change a sprite's costume 10 times at half-second intervals. The result is the generation of animation that makes it look like the bat is flying.

Figure 10.1
The code blocks on the left are displayed when you are working with a sprite, and the code blocks on the right are displayed when you are working with the stage.

To change the costume of the sprite to which this script is added, select the costume's name from the looks block's drop-down list. The block's drop-down list is automatically populated with a list of all of the costumes that have been added to the sprite. The costumes listed in the previous example refer to two costumes representing different views of a bat, as shown in Figure 10.2, and are supplied as part of a collection of graphic files that ships with Scratch.

Costume numbers are automatically assigned by Scratch as you import new costumes into a sprite. The first costume assigned to a sprite is given a costume number of 1. Each successive costume is assigned a higher number, as demonstrated in Figure 10.3.

Using the second looks block shown on the left-hand side of Figure 10.1, you can change a sprite's costume to the next costume in the costume list. For example, the following script automatically changes a sprite's costume whenever the sprite is clicked.

When executed, the script changes the sprite's costume to the next costume in the list. By clicking on the sprite repeatedly, you continue changing the sprite's

Figure 10.2
Bat costumes.

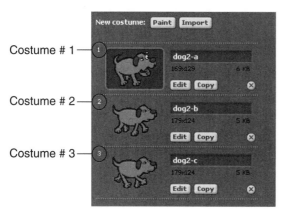

Costume # 1

Costume # 2

Costume # 3

Figure 10.3
Three costumes have been added to a sprite, each of which depicts a slightly different version of a blue dog. These costumes are numbered 1, 2, and 3 and are named dog2-a, dog2-b, and dog2-c, respectively.

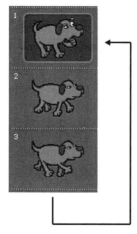

Figure 10.4
Scratch loops back to the beginning of the sprite's costume list as necessary to fulfill additional costume switches.

costume. Once the last costume in the costume list has been displayed, Scratch will go back to the top of the costume list and start over, as depicted in Figure 10.4.

The last looks block shown at bottom left of Figure 10.1 can be used to display a monitor that presents a sprite costume number on the stage. Alternatively, you can use this code block as input to any code block that accepts numeric input.

Changing a Stage's Background Costumes

The looks code blocks on the right-hand side of Figure 10.1 are used to change the stage's background and work identically to their counterparts that deal with costumes. For example, the following script demonstrates how to randomly set the stage's background to one of three options.

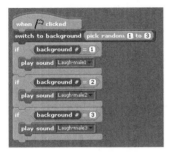

Note that in addition to changing the stage's background twice, this example also plays one of three audio files, depending on which of the three backgrounds is randomly selected.

Making Sprites Talk and Think

The following set of looks code blocks, shown in Figure 10.5, is applicable only to sprites and can used to display text in speech and thought bubbles, making a sprite look like it is talking or thinking.

Figure 10.6 provides examples of how speech and thought bubbles look.

The first two code blocks are used to display text in speech bubbles. The difference between these two code blocks is that the first code block displays its text

Figure 10.5
Using these code blocks, you can display text in both speech and thought bubbles.

Figure 10.6
Speech and thought bubbles resemble callouts used to display captions in cartoons found in many popular newspaper comic strips.

for a specified number of seconds, and the second code block permanently displays its text (until the text is overridden by another speech or thought bubble). For example, the following script could be used to display the text Hello! for two seconds in a speech bubble.

Tip

Any text displayed using the second and fourth code blocks shown in Figure 10.5 do not automatically go away. However, you can clear out the text displayed in a speech or thought bubble by executing a speech or thought code block with no text typed in it.

Similarly, the following script demonstrates how to display a text message of Hmm... in a thought bubble.

Applying Special Effects to Costumes and Backgrounds

The next three looks code blocks, shown in Figure 10.7, apply to both sprites and the stage and can be used to apply and clear different graphical special effects.

The first and second code blocks shown in Figure 10.7 select and then apply one of the following special effects to a sprite's costume or to the stage's background.

- **Color.** Modifies the costume or background's color.

- **Fisheye.** Magnifies a portion of a costume or background.

- **Whirl.** Twists and distorts a portion of a costume or background.

Figure 10.7
These code blocks allow you to set and clear different graphics effects on sprites.

- **Pixelate.** Displays a sprite or background at a lower resolution than the resolution at which the image was created.

- **Mosaic.** Creates an image made up of repeated instances of a sprite or background.

- **Brightness.** Modifies an image by increasing or decreasing its intensity of light.

- **Ghost.** Fades the appearance of a costume or background to make it look transparent.

An example of each of these graphic effects on a sprite is shown in Figure 10.8.

To develop a better understanding of how to work with these two code blocks, let's look at a couple of examples. In this first example, a sprite's appearance is changed by executing a loop four times. Each time the loop executes, it applies the ghost effect to the sprite to which it belongs.

Note that the value specified in the input field for the code block in the previous script is 25, which represents a percentage value. As such, for each of the four times that the loop repeats, the sprite fades away until at the end of the last execution of the loop, the sprite completely disappears.

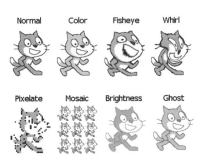

Figure 10.8
A demonstration of how special effects affect a sprite.

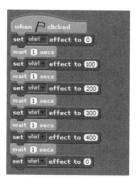

This second example applies the whirl special effect to its sprite. Specifically, it begins by clearing any previous whirl effect that may have been applied to the sprite. Then, over a period of four seconds, it slowly modifies the appearance of the sprite by applying an increased application of the whirl effect. A one-second pause then ensues, and the sprite is returned to its original state.

The last looks code block restores a costume or background back to its original appearance regardless of how many different graphical effects may have been applied to it. For example, the following statement demonstrates how to restore a costume or background's appearance when the green flag button is pressed.

Changing a Sprite's Size

The next three looks code block, shown in Figure 10.9, apply only to sprites. They allow you to change a sprite's size.

The first code block modifies a sprite's size by specifying a relative value. Using this code block, as demonstrated next, you can slowly increase a sprite's size and then reduce its size just as quickly.

Figure 10.9
With these code blocks, you can modify a sprite's size.

The second code block shown in Figure 10.9 lets you set a sprite's size to a specific percentage of its current size (larger or smaller). For example, the following script begins by doubling the size of a sprite. It then pauses for a second and reduces the sprite to 50% of its original size. After another brief pause, the sprite is restored to its original size.

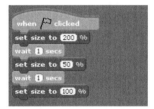

Making Sprites Appear and Disappear

The next two looks code blocks, shown in Figure 10.10, apply only to sprites. As the text displayed on the blocks indicates, they programmatically display or hide a sprite.

Since they do not accept any input, these two code blocks are very easy to work with. For example, the following script can be added to any sprite to make it disappear and then reappear after a one-second pause.

Figure 10.10
With these two code blocks, you can control when sprites appear on the stage.

Determining What Happens when Two Sprites Overlap

The last two Scratch looks code blocks, shown in Figure 10.11, specify what happens when all or part of a sprite is covered by another sprite.

In Scratch, each sprite that you add to an application is assigned to a layer. For example, suppose you create an application with multiple sprites. When you add the first sprite to the application, it is placed at the topmost layer. When you add the application's second sprite, it gets added to the top layer, and the previous sprite gets moved back one layer. Each additional sprite starts off on the top layer and stays there until you either add another new sprite or until you click on one of the sprites that was previously added, which moves the selected sprite back to the topmost layer.

By default, the first sprite would be placed on the top layer. The second sprite added to the application would be placed on the second layer, and the third sprite would be placed on the third layer.

Understanding the layer on which a sprite has been placed is important because the sprite's layer assignment determines whether it remains on top or is displayed underneath another sprite when they overlap one another. Sprites at higher levels remain on top of sprites at lower levels.

Note

To better understand the importance of levels, consider what happens when you place five pieces of paper on top of one another on a desk. The piece of paper sitting on top (at the top layer) is visible, and your view of the other pieces of paper is obstructed. Now, reach into the middle of the stack of paper, pull out a sheet, and place it on top of all the other pages. By altering the page's layer position, you have now made it visible.

In addition to controlling what happens to sprites by adding them to applications in a specific order, controlling their layer position, you can use the code blocks shown in Figure 10.12 to programmatically control a sprite layer location. For example, using the first code block, you can move a sprite to the top layer, ensuring that it remains visible at all times on the stage, even when other sprites come into contact with it.

Figure 10.11
With these code blocks, you can determine what happens when two sprites overlap.

As an example of how to work with both of these code blocks, revisit the Ball Chase game that was presented in Chapter 9, where both of these two code blocks were used to ensure that end of game messages were displayed on top of all other sprites. In addition, the application also used these blocks to ensure that the cat overlaps the ball when it catches it.

Developing the Crazy Eight Ball Game

Now it is time to turn your attention to the development of a new Scratch application, the Crazy Eight Ball game. This game simulates the operation of a crazy eight ball fortune-telling toy. As you work on the development of this game, you will get additional experience with different looks code blocks. In total, the application is made up of three sprites and three scripts. Figure 10.12 shows how the game looks when first started.

To play the game, think of a question and then click on the image of the cat located in the center of the eight ball. Once clicked, the image of the cat is replaced with an 8, as demonstrated in Figure 10.13, and over the next four seconds, the sounds of bubbles can be heard.

Figure 10.12
To play, you must ask questions that can be answered with yes/no-style answers.

Figure 10.13
It takes a few moments for the crazy eight ball to come up with an answer.

Figure 10.14
The crazy eight ball has decided not to answer the player's question.

The crazy eight ball displays any of five randomly selected answers in response to player questions. The range of answers supported by the game includes:

■ Maybe!

■ No!

■ Yes!

■ Ask a different question!

■ Maybe... but then maybe not!

Figure 10.14 shows how the game looks once it has finally decided on an answer to the player's question.

The development of this application project will be created by following a series of steps, as outlined here:

1. Creating a new Scratch application project.

2. Adding and removing sprites.

3. Adding the variable needed by the application.

4. Adding an audio file to the application.

5. Adding a script to control the display of the 8 in the eight ball.

6. Adding the programming logic required to operate the eight ball.

7. Saving and executing your work.

Step 1: Creating a New Scratch Project

Begin the creation of the Crazy Eight Ball game by creating a new Scratch project. The easiest way is to start Scratch, which automatically creates a new application project. Alternatively, if Scratch is already open, create a new application by clicking on the New button located on the Scratch menu bar.

Step 2: Adding and Removing Sprites

The Crazy Eight Ball game consists of three sprites and three scripts, as shown in Figure 10.15.

The first sprite that you need to add to the game is that of an empty eight ball. The second sprite is that of a number 8. You will find copies of graphics for both of these sprites located on this book's companion CD-ROM. You can add these sprites to your new Scratch application by clicking on the Choose New Sprite from File button and then selecting these files. Alternatively, you can create them yourself by clicking on the Paint New Sprite button and then using the Paint Editor program. Once added to the stage, reposition these two sprites so that the eight ball is centered in the middle of the stage and the number is centered in the middle of the eight ball.

The application's third sprite is that of a cat's face. You can create this sprite by using the Paint Editor program to edit the application's default sprite, removing the Cat sprite's body, leaving just its face in place. Once modified, click on the

Figure 10.15
An overview of the different components that make up the Crazy Eight Ball game.

Figure 10.16
The Crazy Eight Ball game requires one variable.

Grow Sprite button located on Scratch's toolbar and then click on the image of the Cat sprite 12 times to increase the size of the cat's face. Next, reposition the Cat sprite, moving it onto the center of the eight ball so that it overlaps the Cat sprite. At this point, the overall design of the Crazy Eight Ball game is complete.

Before moving on to the next step, rename these three sprites Cat, EightBall, and Number, as shown in Figure 10.15.

Step 3: Adding a Variable Required by the Application

In order to execute, the Crazy Eight Ball game requires the definition of the variable shown in Figure 10.16. To add this variable, click on the Variables button located at the top of the blocks palette, click on the Make a Variable button, and create a new variable named RandomNo.

This variable will be used to store a randomly generated number that the game will use when generating answers to player questions.

Step 4: Adding an Audio File to the Application

The Crazy Eight Ball game makes use of a single sound effect, which sounds like bubbles being blown in water. This sound is played for four seconds preceding the display of the eight ball's answer. The audio file that is played must be added to the Cat sprite. To add this sound file, select the Cat sprite thumbnail in the sprite list and then click on the Sounds tab located at the top of the scripts area. Next, click on the Import button to display the Import Sound window, double-click on the Effects folder, select the Bubbles audio file, and then click on OK.

Step 5: Creating a Script to Control the Display of the 8 in the Eight Ball

Of the application's three scripts, two belong to the Number sprite. These scripts, shown next, are automatically executed based on the receipt of broadcast messages.

Specifically, when a message of Show 8 is received, the Eight sprite is made visible. When the message Hide 8 is received, the Eight sprite is hidden. The receipt of these messages serves as triggers, which control when the Eight sprite is visible (which only occurs when the eight ball is in the process of preparing to generate an answer).

As you can see, these two scripts each use a looks code block to control sprite visibility. Since the game begins by displaying only the image of the Cat sprite, go ahead and click on the second script belonging to the Eight sprite, hiding it from view.

Step 6: Adding the Programming Logic Needed to Control the Eight Ball

The last script in the application, shown next, belongs to the Cat sprite. It is executed whenever the player thinks of a question and clicks on the Cat sprite for an answer.

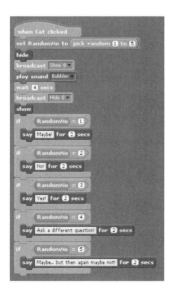

Once started, the script begins by assigning a random number in the range of 1 to 5 to the RandomNo variable. Next, a looks code block is executed, hiding the Cat sprite and then the broadcast message Show 8 is sent. This message will trigger the execution of a script belonging to the Eight sprite. Next, the Bubbles audio file is played, and the script's execution is paused for four seconds, allowing Scratch time to finish playing the audio file. Once the four seconds is up, a second broadcast message of Hide 8 is sent, triggering the hiding of the Eight sprite.

Next, the Cat sprite is redisplayed on the stage and the value assigned to RandomNo is analyzed. Depending on the value assigned to RandomNo, one of five different text messages is displayed in a speech bubble. After two seconds, the bubble is closed, and the game waits on the player to ask another question.

Step 7: Saving and Executing Your Scratch Project

At this point, you have all of the information you need to create your own copy of the Crazy Eight Ball game. As long as you followed along carefully with the instructions provided in this chapter, you should not run into any problems. If you have not done so yet, save your new Scratch application project and then switch over to Presentation mode and test it.

Summary

In this chapter, you learned how to work with Scratch's looks code blocks. This included learning how to switch between sprite costumes and different stage backgrounds and how to apply a range of special effects to sprites and backgrounds. You learned how to display text in speech and thought bubbles, control the size of sprites, and programmatically control sprite visibility. You also learned about the importance of understanding layering and how it affects the display of sprites. This chapter also guided you through the creation of the Crazy Eight Ball game.

CHAPTER 11

SPICING THINGS UP WITH SOUNDS

Many different types of applications, especially computer games, rely on sound as a means of conveying meaning and excitement. Through the addition of background music and sound effects, applications can really come alive, providing users with a deeper and more meaningful experience. In Scratch, sound effects and music are integrated into applications using sound blocks. This chapter will teach you how to work with all of Scratch's sound blocks and demonstrate how to incorporate audio files, drum notes, and musical notes into your applications. On top of all this, you will learn how to create a new application called the Family Picture Movie, which demonstrates how to create a slideshow complete with accompanying background music.

The major topics covered in this chapter include learning how to

- Control the playback of audio files

- Play drum beats and pause drum play

- Set and control the volume at which audio files, notes, and musical instruments are played

- Set and change the tempo of drum and note play

Playing Sounds

To add the playback of music and sound effects to your applications, you need to learn how to use the sound code blocks shown in Figure 11.1. These code blocks provide everything you need to play or stop the playback of MP3 and wave files in your Scratch applications.

N o t e

A *wave* file is a type of file designed for storing an audio bit stream on personal computers. Wave files have a .wav file extension. An *MP3* file is an audio file that utilizes advanced compression technology while retaining high audio quality.

The first two code blocks shown in Figure 11.1 let you play any MP3 or wave file that you add to your Scratch project. The third code block lets you stop the playback of all of the audio files belonging to a sprite. In order to play an audio file, you must first add it to a sprite or to the stage, which you can do by selecting the stage or a sprite from the sprite list, clicking on the Sounds tab location at the top of the scripts area, then clicking on the Import button. Once the file is imported, you can play the audio file using a script belonging to the stage or sprite, as demonstrated here.

In Figure 11.2, an audio file named meow is played when the green flag button is pressed. In order to play the audio file, you must select it from the code block's drop-down list. The drop-down list is automatically populated by Scratch with all the audio files that have been added to the sprite to which the script belongs.

The sound code block used in the previous script allows the script to which it has been added to continue running. If the script containing the sound block

Figure 11.1
These code blocks control audio file playback.

Figure 11.2
The meow audio file is played when the green flag button is clicked.

has additional code left to be executed, the playback of the sound will be cut short when the script continues executing. This was not a problem in the previous example because the sound block was the last code block in the script.

For situations where you want to pause script execution to allow time for the entire audio file to finish playing, you have two choices. First, you can add a control block to the script immediately following the sound block that pauses script execution for a specified number of seconds (the number of seconds needed to play the audio file). Better yet, you can use the second code block shown in Figure 11.1 as demonstrated in the following script:

The sound code block used in this example plays an audio file that has been previously added to your Scratch application, pausing script execution until the audio file has finished playing. Once playback is complete, the rest of the script is permitted to finish its execution.

Tip

If you want to add the repeated playback of background music or sound effects to an application, create a script specifically for this purpose. This keeps the programming logic needed to play the audio file separate from other scripts and eliminates the need to pause other scripts' execution to support audio playback.

Depending on what your applications are designed to do, there may be times when you want to stop the playback of audio files belonging to a sprite or the stage. This can be achieved using the third code block shown in Figure 11.1, as demonstrated in the following example:

Here, the playback of any audio files belonging to the sprite is immediately halted when the spacebar is pressed.

Note

In addition to playing any of the audio files supplied with Scratch, you can import external audio files, both MP3 and wave, into any sprite. If your computer has a microphone, you can record your own audio files by selecting a sprite or the stage, clicking on the Sounds tab located at the top of the scripts area, and then clicking on the Record button. This opens the Sound Recorder program shown in Figure 11.3. To record a custom sound, just click on the red Record button, and when you are done, click on OK. Once done, your new audio file will be displayed on the Sounds tab immediately available to your application.

Figure 11.3
Scratch makes it easy to record your own custom audio files.

Play a Drum

Using the two code blocks shown in Figure 11.4, you can add the playing of a drum to your Scratch application and, when necessary, pause drum play for a specified number of beats.

The first code block shown in Figure 11.4 plays a drum sound for a specified number of beats. This code block lets you choose from among 46 different types of drums, each of which is easily selected by clicking on the code block's drop-down list, as demonstrated in Figure 11.5.

The second code block shown in Figure 11.4 lets you momentarily pause drum play for a specified number of beats. Using both of the code blocks, you can play a wide assortment of drums within your applications.

Figure 11.4
These code blocks let you control the playing of a drum within your applications.

Figure 11.5
This code block supports the playing of 46 different types of drum sounds, numbered from 35 to 81.

In this example, the first sound block plays a drum beat for five beats using an Acoustic Snare. The second sound block rests for .5 beats, and the third code block uses an Open Triangle to play a drum for .5 beats.

Playing Musical Notes

In addition to playing audio files and different types of drum beats, Scratch lets you play musical notes with various instruments using the sound code blocks shown in Figure 11.6.

The first code block plays a note for a particular number of beats. You can specify a note either by typing it into the code block's first input box or by clicking on the drop-down list located inside the code block's input field, which displays a graphic representation of a piano keyboard. Using this keyboard, you can select a note by clicking on one of the keyboard keys, as demonstrated in Figure 11.7. The range of available notes is from 0 to 127, with 60 representing the middle C note.

The second code block shown in Figure 11.6 specifies the instrument to be used and is designed to be used in conjunction with the first control block. It supports a total of 128 different instruments, numbered 1 to 128. You can select an

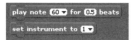

Figure 11.6
These sound blocks let you play notes using musical instruments.

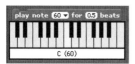

Figure 11.7
Selecting a note is as easy as clicking on a piano key.

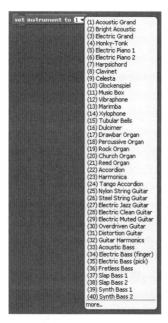

Figure 11.8
Selecting the instrument you want play within your Scratch application.

instrument by keying its number into the block's input field or by selecting an instrument from the block's drop-down list, as demonstrated in Figure 11.8.

The following script demonstrates how to use both of the code blocks shown in Figure 11.6 to play a C note followed by a D note using a harpsichord. Each note is played for .5 beats.

Configuring Audio Volume

Rather than playing audio files, drum beats, and musical notes at whatever volume the computer is set to, you can use the sound code blocks shown in Figure 11.9 to change or set the volume at which audio files, drum beats, and musical notes are played.

The first code block shown in Figure 11.9 is used to change the volume of sound playback for an individual sprite. Using this code block, you can change a sprite's volume by a specified percentage, with 0 being no volume and 100 being the maximum volume. The second code block lets you assign a specific value to a sprite in the range of 0 to 100. Using the third code block, you can retrieve a sprite's volume and optionally display this value in a monitor on the stage.

Note

Volume is set individually for each sprite in an application. Therefore, you can assign different volume levels to each sprite in your application.

An example of how to work with the first of these control blocks is provided here:

Here, an audio file named meow is played at the computer's default volume level. Next, the volume setting for the sprite to which the script has been added is

Figure 11.9
Using these code blocks, you can take control of the volume of music and sound effects played by any sprite in your application.

reduced by 80%. The meow file is then played a second time, this time much quieter.

In this next example, the sprite's volume is set to 10 percent of its default volume level, after which an audio file named meow is played.

Note

The third code block shown in Figure 11.9 can be used to retrieve a sprite's current volume level. In addition, by selecting its check box, you can enable a monitor that displays the volume level of the sprite on the stage.

Setting and Changing Tempo

The last three looks blocks provided by Scratch are shown in Figure 11.10. Using these blocks you can set, change, and report on the tempo at which drum beats and musical notes are played.

The first code block shown in Figure 11.10 changes the tempo used to play a drum or note. *Tempo* is a measurement of the speed, in beats per minute, at which a drum or note is played. The larger the tempo value, the faster the drum or note is played. The second code block lets you set the tempo used to play a drum or note to a specific number of beats per second. Using the third code block, you can retrieve a sprite's currently assigned tempo and optionally display this value in a monitor on the stage.

The following script demonstrates how to set and modify a sprite's tempo when playing musical notes:

Figure 11.10
These code blocks allow you to modify and report on the tempo used by a sprite to play beats and notes.

Here, the tempo used to play notes is set to 60 beats per minute, and then, after a one-second pause, a C note is played five times in a row, each time for a half a beat. After another one-second pause, the sprite's tempo is slowed down by 20 beats per minute, and another C note is played five times.

Creating the Family Picture Movie

The rest of this chapter is dedicated to showing you how to develop your next application project, the Family Picture Movie. The development of this application provides the opportunity to work further with different sound blocks, controlling sound volume, playback, and playback termination. In total, the application will be made up of 8 sprites and 13 scripts. Figure 11.11 shows how the application looks when initially started.

To run the application and view its picture show, all you have to do is click on the green flag button. Once clicked, the application begins an animation sequence that counts down from five and then starts displaying a series of pictures representing the contents of the movie, as demonstrated in Figure 11.12.

Background music is played to help set a friendly tone as the pictures are displayed. The Family Picture Movie is capable of displaying any number of pictures. Once the movie ends, credits are displayed, as shown in Figure 11.13.

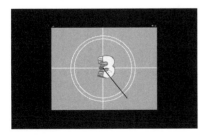

Figure 11.11
The application begins by displaying a series of numbers, from 5 to 1, on an orange radar screen.

Figure 11.12
As the movie plays, a series of pictures is displayed at three-second intervals.

Figure 11.13
Credits are displayed at the end of the movie.

The development of this project will be created by following a series of steps, as outlined here:

1. Creating a new Scratch project.

2. Adding and removing sprites and backgrounds.

3. Adding the variable needed by the application.

4. Adding an audio file to the application.

5. Adding the programming logic to control application execution.

6. Saving and executing your work.

Step 1: Creating a New Scratch Project

To begin the development of the Family Picture Movie, you must create a new Scratch project. If Scratch is not already running, start it up, and you will be ready to go. Otherwise, if you already have Scratch open, click on the New button located on the Scratch menu bar, and a new project will be created for you.

Figure 11.14
An overview of the different components that make up the Family Picture Movie application.

Step 2: Adding and Removing Sprites and Backgrounds

The Family Picture Movie is made up of 8 sprites and 13 scripts, as shown in Figure 11.14.

The application consists of two separate backgrounds: Counter, which is displayed when the application is first started and begins its countdown, and the default blank stage background. A copy of the Counter background can be found on this book's companion CD. To add it, click on the Stage thumbnail located on the sprite list and then click on the Backgrounds tab located at the top of the scripts area. Next, click on the Import button and use the Import Background window to locate and select the Counter background file. Since the Counter background is going to be used as the application's initial background, drag and drop its thumbnail from the bottom of the list of background files to the top position.

In addition to the background, the Family Picture Movie makes use of a number of sprites. As shown in Figure 11.15, the first of these sprites is a black line. You can create this sprite yourself using the Paint Editor program, or you can import the Line sprite located on this book's companion CD. To add this sprite, click on the Choose New Sprite from File button, opening the New Sprite window, and then locate and import the sprite. Once the sprite is added, you need to position it exactly as shown in Figure 11.14.

Note

If you elect to create your own version of the Line sprite, you will need to set the rotation center for the sprite as shown in Figure 11.15.

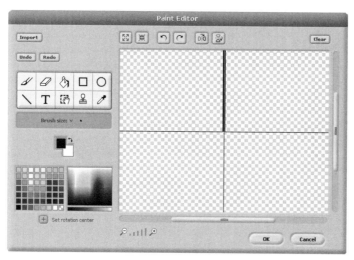

Figure 11.15
Assigning a rotation center to the Line sprite.

Next, you need to add five sprites representing numbers displayed during the application's opening animation sequence. To add the first of these five numbers, click on the Choose New Sprite from File button and then drill down into the Letters folder followed by the Stone folder. Next, select the 5 sprite and click on the OK button. As you will see, the sprite is colored black and white. However, it is supposed to be red and yellow. To fix this, you need to edit the sprite and change its colors. To do this, select the thumbnail representing the sprite and then click on the Costumes tab located at the top of the scripts area. Next, select the sprite's thumbnail and click on its Edit button, opening it in the Paint Editor program. Using the Fill tool located in the Paint Editor's toolbar, modify the black portions of the sprite and make them red. Then modify all of the white portions of the sprite, making them yellow. Using the steps outlined above, add the 4, 3, 2, and 1 sprites to the application, editing each one so that they are red and yellow.

Once the initial animation sequence has finished, the Family Picture Movie begins displaying a series of graphics pictures. To add the first of these pictures, click on the Choose New Sprite from File button and then add any graphic files that you want. If you do not have a suitable graphic file handy, you can use the

Pics file located on this book's companion CD. The rest of the pictures shown in the application will be displayed by changing this sprite's costume. To add additional costumes to the sprite, select the sprite, click on the Costumes tab located at the top of the scripts area, and then click on the Import button, opening the Import Costume window. If you do not have any suitable pictures to be used as backgrounds, you can import the background files provided on this book's companion CD. These background files have names like IM000327.

The last sprite to be added to the application is a graphic file that displays the application's credits. You can create and add your own sprite using the Paint Editor program, or you can import the Credits sprite located on this book's companion CD. Once this sprite has been added, the stage should be filled with different sprites. However, of all of these sprites, only the Line sprite needs to remain visible. To temporarily remove each of the remaining sprites from view, select each sprite one at a time, click on the Looks button located at the top of the blocks palette, and then double-click on the Hide code block. By the time you are done, the stage should look like the example shown in Figure 11.14.

Step 3: Adding a Variable Required by the Application

In order to execute, the Family Picture Movie requires that you define a single variable. To add this variable, click on the Variables button located at the top of the blocks palette, click on the Make a Variable button, and then create a new variable named Counter, as shown in Figure 11.16.

The application will use the variable to control the execution of the application's opening countdown sequence, coordinating the display of the numbers used during the countdown process.

Step 4: Adding an Audio File to the Application

As it executes, the Family Picture Movie plays background music to set the mood for the application. The script responsible for playing this music belongs to the Pics sprite. To add this audio file to the Pics sprite, select the sprite's thumbnail

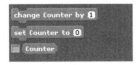

Figure 11.16
The Family Picture Movie uses one variable to help control the opening animation sequence.

in the sprite list and then click on the Sounds tab located at the top of the scripts area. Next, click on the Import button to display the Import Sound window, double-click on the Music Loops folder, select the GuitarChords2 audio file, and then click on OK.

Step 5: Developing the Application's Programming Logic

The programming logic that drives the execution of the Family Picture Movie is organized into 13 separate scripts, assigned to each of the application's sprites and to its background. The overall execution of all of this application's scripts is coordinated through the use of broadcast messages and through the use of control blocks that monitor the value assigned to the application's variable, executing only when the variable reaches a predefined value.

Setting Up the Opening Animation Sequence

The Family Picture Movie begins running when the player clicks on the green flag button. When this occurs, a number of the scripts within the application begin executing. One of these scripts is responsible for managing the animated sequence that plays when the application first begins executing. This script, shown next, must be added to the Line sprite.

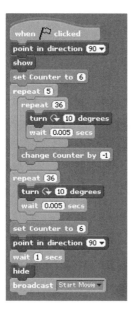

As you can see, this script begins by setting the direction of the Line sprite and then makes it visible. Next, the Counter variable is assigned a starting value of 6, after which a loop is set up to execute five times. Within this loop, a second loop executes 36 times (for a total of 360 degrees), rotating the Line sprite by 10 degrees and pausing .005 second after each turn. The value assigned to Counter is then decremented by a value of −1.

By the time the outer loop has executed five times, five other application scripts, monitoring the value assigned to Counter, are executed. Each of these five scripts is responsible for displaying a number on the stage. The end result is an animated sequence that emulates the countdown that is often displayed at the beginning of old movie reels. Once the countdown has been completed, a second loop executes, rotating the Line sprite one final time around the center of the stage. Once the last loop has finished, the value of Counter is reset to 6 and pointed back to its initial direction. A one-second pause then ensues, and the Line sprite is hidden. Lastly, a control block is used to send a broadcast message of Start Movie. This broadcast message will be used to trigger the execution of two scripts belonging to the Pics sprite, which is responsible for displaying the pictures that make up the application's picture show.

Displaying the Numeric Countdown

As the previous script executes, it modifies the value assigned to the Counter variable, changing its value from 6 to 1, one number at a time. Each of the five sprites representing the numbers displayed during the opening animation sequence is displayed by scripts belonging to those sprites. The scripts belonging to each sprite are nearly identical. The following script belongs to the Sprite5 sprite:

As you can see, it starts executing when the player clicks on the green flag button, which begins by making sure that the sprite is hidden from view. The script then goes into a loop that waits until the value of Counter is set to 5. Once this occurs, the script displays the sprite for 1.6 seconds and then hides it again. After creating this script, drag and drop an instance of it onto the Sprite4, Sprite3, Sprite2, and Sprite1 sprites and then modify the scripts belonging to each sprite by changing the value that is looked for to 4, 3, 2, and 1, respectively.

Switching Costumes and Playing Background Music

As has been previously stated, the application displays different pictures by changing costumes. In addition, background music is played to help set the mood as the picture show begins. Two separate scripts, belonging to the Pics sprite, are responsible for managing the switching of costumes and the playing of the application's audio file. Both of the scripts are automatically executed when the Start Movie broadcast message is received.

The first of these two scripts, shown next, manages costume switches. It begins by displaying a default costume of IM000327, which is then displayed on the stage. Next a loop is set up that pauses three seconds and then switches the sprite's costume to the next costume in the list.

The second script, shown next, begins by sending out its broadcast message of Clear background and then sets the sprite's value to half its current level. Next, a loop is set up that executes 10 times. Each time the loop executes, an audio file named GuitarChords2 is played. At the end of its tenth execution, the loop halts, and the Pics sprite is hidden. The script ends by sending out a broadcast message of Show Credits.

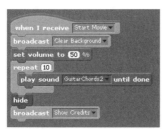

Note

The `Show Credits` broadcast message is used as a trigger that executes a script belonging to the `Credits` sprite.

Displaying the Closing Credits

The `Credits` sprite has two scripts, as shown next. The first script executes when the green flag button is pressed and is responsible for removing the display of the sprite from the stage.

The second script is automatically executed when the `Show Credits` broadcast message is received. It displays the `Credits` sprite, waits three seconds, and then hides the sprite, leaving the stage blank. The script ends by executing a control block that halts the execution of the application's scripts.

Switching Backgrounds

The last two scripts belong to the stage. These scripts are shown next. The first script executes when the green flag button is clicked. Its job is to switch the stage's background to `Counter`, readying the application to begin its five-second countdown sequence.

The second of the stage's scripts automatically executes when the `Clear Background` broadcast message is received. Once executed, it switches the stage back to the default `Clear` background.

Step 6: Saving and Executing Your Scratch Project

Assuming you have followed along carefully with the instructions that have been provided, your copy of the Family Picture Movie should be ready for testing. If you have not already saved your new application, do so now. When you are ready, click on the green flag button to run the application and watch the movie. In the event that you run into any problems, go back and recheck your work against the instructions outlined in this chapter.

Summary

The addition of sound playback is fundamental to the operation of many Scratch applications. In Scratch, sound effects and music playback are controlled through different sound code blocks. Using these code blocks, you can convey additional meaning and enhance excitement when your applications run. This chapter provided instruction on how to work with all of Scratch's sound blocks and to use them to play audio files, drum notes, and musical notes. You also learned how to change the tempo at which drums and notes are played; control the volumes at which audio files, notes, and drum beats are played; and select different types of drums and instruments to be played.

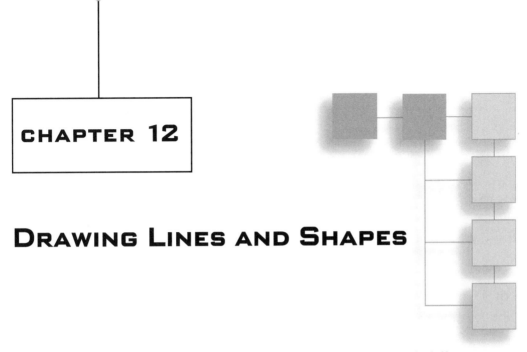

CHAPTER 12

DRAWING LINES AND SHAPES

In addition to displaying sprites with different costumes and different stage backgrounds, Scratch also draws custom lines, shapes, and other graphics using pen code blocks. Using a virtualized pen, these blocks allow you to set the color, width, and shade used in drawing operations. This chapter reveals how to work with all of Scratch's pen blocks and will end by demonstrating how to use them to create a paint drawing application.

The major topics covered in this chapter include learning how to:

- Draw using Scratch's virtual pen
- Set the color used when drawing
- Set pen shade and size
- Stamp a copy of a costume on the stage
- Clear the stage of any drawing operations

Clearing the Stage Area

The first of Scratch's pen code blocks, shown in Figure 12.1, is designed to let you clear out any drawing operations that you may have made on the stage.

Figure 12.1
This pen block is used to clear out any drawing operations that you may have made on the stage.

Anything you draw or stamp on the stage's current costume does not actually change the costume. Therefore, when you clear out any drawing, the costume that makes up the background remains unchanged. The following script demonstrates how easy it is to use this code block:

By adding a script like this to a Scratch application, you can reset the stage back to its original state (erasing any drawing made to the stage).

Drawing with the Pen

Within Scratch applications, drawing is performed using a virtual pen. This pen works very much like a real pen. When placed in a down position, it can be used to draw on the stage. When placed in an up position, drawing ceases. In order to draw or stop drawing, you must be able to programmatically control the pen's up and down positions, which you can do using the code blocks shown in Figure 12.2.

Using the first code block, you can easily create a simple drawing application. To create this application, start a new Scratch project and then delete the default cat sprite and replace it with a new sprite made up of a small black dot (easily created using the Paint Editor program). Once you have created your new application as described above, select its sprite and add the following script to it:

Figure 12.2
Using these pen blocks, you can control when the pen can be used to draw.

When executed, this script clears the stage and then places Scratch's virtual pen in a down position, enabling drawing to occur (whenever the sprite to which the script belongs is moved). Next, a loop is set up that uses a motion block to make the sprite follow the pointer around the stage. As a result, whenever you move the mouse around the stage, the sprite follows, and a line is drawn. Once you create and run your own copy of this application, it should become immediately clear that you do not have enough control over the pen. Specifically, you cannot control when and when not to draw. This situation is easily remedied by modifying the script so that you can place the pen in a down or up position based on the status of the mouse-pointer's left-mouse button, as shown next.

Figure 12.3 shows an example of a picture drawn on the stage using this modified version of the application. By being able to control when the pen is in a down position, you can produce a precise drawing.

Figure 12.3
A quick little doodle created using a small drawing application.

Setting Pen Color

In addition to being able to clear the stage and control when the pen is up or down, Scratch also specifies the color that is used in drawing operations using any of the three pen code blocks shown in Figure 12.4.

The first code block shown in Figure 12.4 lets you set the color to be used when drawing by allowing you to click on the color swatch located in its input field. When the swatch is clicked, Scratch responds by displaying a color palette, as shown in Figure 12.5. You can select the color you want either by clicking on the color shown within the color palette or by moving the pointer, which now looks like a dropper, over any color currently displayed anywhere on the Scratch IDE and clicking in it. Once specified, the color you selected is displayed in the code block's input area.

The following script demonstrates how to use this code block to specify the color you want to use.

Here, the stage is cleared, and the pen's color is set to red. Otherwise, the application operates no differently than before.

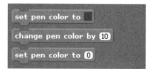

Figure 12.4
The code blocks let you control the color used when drawing.

Figure 12.5
Select a color by clicking anywhere on the color palette.

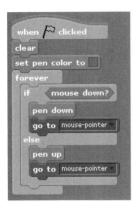

Scratch also lets you specify the color to be used when drawing by specifying a number. For example, the following list identifies numbers that you can use to specify a range of commonly used colors.

- 0 = red

- 20 = orange

- 35 = yellow

- 70 = green

- 130 = blue

- 150 = purple

- 175 = pink

By experimenting with other numbers, you identify a host of different colors. For example, using the second code block shown in Figure 12.4, you change the color used when drawing, changing it relative to its currently assigned value.

Here, the pen block has been added to the beginning of the script's loop. Each time the loop repeats, it changes the pen's current color assignment by a value of 10. The result is that a rainbow effect is applied as you draw, with the color changing across a full spectrum supported by Scratch as you move the mouse and draw on the stage.

Using the third code block shown in Figure 12.4, you can specify the color to be used when drawing using its associated numeric value. For example, you could modify the application's script to draw using red with this code block by passing it a value of 0, as demonstrated here.

Changing Pen Shade

In addition to selecting color, Scratch also allows you to select the level of shading applied when drawing. The range of values supported by the pen shade is 1 to 100, as demonstrated in Figure 12.6.

By default, Scratch applies a shading value of 50 when drawing colors. A shade value of 0 results in a black color. A shade value of 100 results in white. Scratch lets you specify the level of shading to be applied when drawing using either of the pen code blocks shown in Figure 12.7.

0   100

Figure 12.6
Shading affects the application of light to a color.

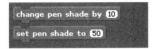

Figure 12.7
You can change the value used to apply shading by varying its current value or by setting an entirely new value.

As an example of how to work with the first code block shown in Figure 12.7, let's modify the drawing example again as shown here.

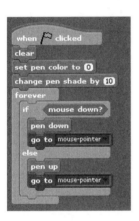

Here, the shading level has been increased by a value of 10. Rather than change the shading level relative to its current value, you can use the second code block shown in Figure 12.7 to specify a shade level, as demonstrated in the following script:

Working with Different Size Pens

In addition to setting color and shading values, Scratch also lets you change the size of the pen. This can be accomplished using either of the two pen code blocks shown in Figure 12.8.

By default, Scratch draws using a pen size of 1. You can change the pen size relative to its current size using the first code block, as demonstrated in the following script:

Here, the size of the pen used in the drawing application in increased by 1, making it twice its default size. If you prefer, you can simply assign a specific pen size using the second code block, as demonstrated here.

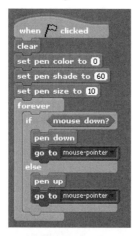

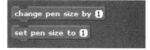

Figure 12.8
Scratch supports an unlimited number of pen sizes.

Figure 12.9
An example of a drawing made using a pen size of 10.

In this example, the drawing application has been modified to use a pen that's size has been increased to 10. Figure 12.9 shows an example of a simple drawing created using the application with this pen size.

Stamping an Instance of a Costume on the Stage

In addition to all of the pen code blocks demonstrated so far, Scratch provides one last block, shown in Figure 12.10, which allows you to capture a sprite's costume and use it to stamp copies of the sprite on the stage.

As an example of how to work with this code block, create a new Scratch application, remove the default cat sprite from it, and then add a copy of the crab1-a sprite to it. You will find this sprite in Scratch's Animals folder. Once added, shrink the sprite down to about a third of its default size and then add the following script to it.

Figure 12.10
This code block lets you use a sprite's costume as the basis for creating a stamp.

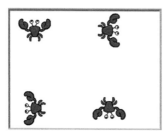

Figure 12.11
Decorating the stage using a sprite as the basis for generating stamps.

When executed, this script clears the stage of any previous drawing, which also includes stamps, moves the sprite to the upper-left corner of the stage, and sets its direction. Next, a loop is executed four times, stamping the image of the sprite four times as it is moved around the stage. Figure 12.11 shows how the stage will look once the script has finished executing.

Creating the Doodle Drawing Application

At this point you have completed your review of all of Scratch's code blocks and have learned how to put them all to work. Now it is time to work on the chapter's application project, the Doodle Drawing application. This paint-like application expands on the examples you have been working on throughout this chapter, making extensive use of the pen code blocks and allowing you to draw by selecting from a range of predefined colors. The application allows you to draw using a range of different pen sizes. There is also a Clear feature that lets you start over any time you want so that you can begin working on a new drawing.

In total, the Doodle Drawing application is made up of 12 sprites and 3 scripts. Figure 12.12 shows how the game looks when first started.

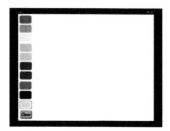

Figure 12.12
Drawings are made by holding down the left mouse button and moving the mouse-pointer around the stage.

Figure 12.13
You can use any of 10 colors and 9 different pen sizes when drawing.

To create a drawing, click on one of buttons shown on the left-hand side of the stage to pick a color, then hold down the mouse's left button, and move the mouse-pointer around the stage. If you want, you can use different-sized lines when drawing by pressing keyboard keys 1 through 9. Pressing the 1 key results in a thin line, whereas pressing the 9 key results in a line that is approximately a quarter-of-an-inch thick. If you make a mistake or want to start over, you can do so at any time by clicking on the Clear button located at the lower-left side of the stage.

Figure 12.13 shows the Doodle Drawing application in action. Here, the application has been used to draw a snowman, complete with a blue hat and red scarf.

The development of this application project will be created by following a series of steps, as outlined here:

1. Creating a new Scratch application project.

2. Adding and removing sprites.

3. Developing the application programming logic.

4. Saving and executing your work.

Step 1: Creating a New Scratch Project

To begin work on the Doodle Drawing application, you need to create a new Scratch project. If Scratch is already running, click on the New button located on the Scratch menu bar. Otherwise, start Scratch up, and it will automatically create a new application for you to work on.

Step 2: Adding and Removing Sprites

The Doodle Drawing application is made up of 12 sprites and 3 scripts, as shown in Figure 12.14.

This application does not need the default cat sprite, so you should begin by removing that sprite from the application. The first 10 sprites that you need to add to the application represent the application button controls. To add the first of these controls, click on the Choose New Sprite from File button and drill down in to the Things folder where the New Sprite window appears. Next, locate and select the button sprite and then click on OK. Once it has been added to the stage, drag and drop this sprite to the upper-left corner of the stage, click on the Costumes tab located at the top of the scripts area, and then click on the sprite's Edit button.

Using the Fill tool feature located on the Paint Editor's toolbar, change the entire surface of the sprite to red. This will take a number of different clicks because the sprite has many shaded areas and cannot therefore be filled with red in a single click. Once you have completed this task, click on the Paint Editor's OK button and then rename the sprite Red.

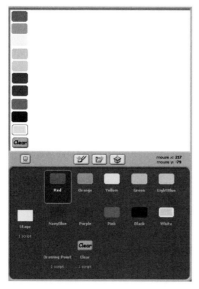

Figure 12.14
An overview of the different parts of the Doodle Drawing application.

Now that the first of the 10 button sprites has been created, things will go a lot faster. Right-click on the Red sprite and select Duplicate from the popup menu that appears. Rename the new sprite Orange and then click on the Edit button located in the Costumes tab. Using the Fill tool control, make the button orange and then click on OK. Now, reposition the Orange sprite so that it lines up just under the Red sprite. Using the steps outlined in this paragraph, create eight more buttons for the following colors.

- Yellow

- Green

- LightBlue

- NavyBlue

- Purple

- Pink

- Black

- White

Next, you need to add a small sprite in the shape of a black dot to the application. To do so, click on the Paint New Sprite button and then when the Paint Editor appears, click once on its canvas to make a black dot and then click on the OK button. Rename this sprite Drawing Point. Now, add the last sprite using the same steps you used to add the application's first button. Once added, click on the Edit button located on the Costumes tab and using the Text tool feature located on the Paint Editor's toolbar, add the word Clear on top of the button (using the ComicSans font with a font size of 14). Click on the OK button when you are done and rename the sprite Clear and then reposition the sprite so that it appears as the final button on the lower-right side of the stage.

The default blank background will be used in this application to provide it with white space on which to draw. Assuming that you have created all of the sprites as instructed above, you should be ready to begin the coding process.

Step 3: Creating Scripts Used to Control the Doodle Drawing Application

Most of the Doodle Drawing application's programming logic resides within a single script belonging to the Drawing Point sprite. This script is responsible for all drawing operations, including determining which color and what size pen the user wants to use. The remaining logic revolves around the clearing of the stage, which is handled by two small scripts, one belonging to the Clear sprite and the other to the stage.

Developing the Drawing Point Sprite's Programming Logic

The programming logic that controls the overall execution of all drawing within the Doodle Drawing application belongs to a script that must be added to the Drawing Point sprite. Do not let the length of the code deceive you; the programming logic is really very simple.

To help make things easy to follow, the script will be developed in three parts. For the first part, create and add the following script to the Drawing Point sprite:

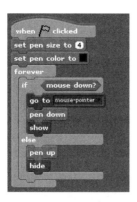

As you can see, the script executes when the green flag button is pressed. It starts by setting a default pen size of 4 and a default color of black. Next, a loop is set up that will be used to manage the execution of all of the remaining code blocks. The first set of code blocks to be embedded within the loop is already present. It consists of a control block that checks to see if the left mouse button is being pressed, and if it is, the Drawing Point sprite is moved to the mouse-pointer, the pen is placed in a down position, and the Drawing Point sprite is displayed. If the left mouse button is not being pressed, then the pen is placed in an up position and the Drawing Point sprite is hidden from view.

The programming logic outlined above is responsible for the overall management of the drawing process and is in fact all that is needed to create a simple drawing application. If you want, you can switch to Presentation mode and run the application and use it to draw. Of course, as currently written, the application only allows the user to draw using a color of black and a pen size of 4. To enhance the application so that the user can select different colors by clicking on one of the color buttons located on the left-hand side of the stage, add the following code block to the end of the script, placing it inside and at the bottom of the script's loop.

As you can see, the code blocks shown previously are organized using 10 separate conditional code blocks, each of which checks to see if the Drawing Point sprite has been moved over one of the 10 color buttons. (In order for the sprite to be moved over one of the buttons, the Drawing Point sprite must be visible, which occurs only when the left mouse button is pressed.) If it has, then the pen's color is changed to reflect the button the user has clicked.

Note

The application only switches color when the Drawing Point sprite is moved over a color button and the left mouse button is clicked. The Drawing Point must be visible for this to work, and this is the case only when the left mouse button is being pressed. Therefore, to select a color, the user must click on the color. Simply moving the mouse over a color will not select it.

In addition to allowing the user to choose a color by clicking on one of the application's 10 color button controls, the application also allows the user to change pen size by clicking on keyboard keys 1 through 9. To enable support for different pen sizes, add the following code block to the script, inside and at the bottom of the script's loop.

As you can see, these code blocks are organized using nine separate conditional control blocks, each of which monitors the keyboard looking for a specific key to be pressed and changing pen size accordingly.

Clearing the Stage

In addition to facilitating drawing using different colors and pen sizes, the Doodle Drawing application also allows the user to clear the stage at any time to ready it for a new drawing. The programming logic that allows the user to clear the stage to start a new drawing is managed by the Clear sprite in conjunction with the stage. The process of clearing the stage is initiated whenever the user clicks on the Clear sprite. When this happens, the following script, which needs to be added to the Clear sprite, is executed.

As you can see, all that this script does is send a broadcast message of Clear, indicating that the user wants to clear the stage. This broadcast message serves as a trigger that initiates the execution of the following script, which must be added to the stage:

As you can see, this script is very straightforward. It executes a pen code block that clears off the stage whenever the Clear broadcast message is received.

Step 4: Saving and Executing Your Scratch Project

All right! You now have all of the information needed to create and execute the Doodle Drawing application. Assuming that you followed along carefully with all of the instructions that were provided, you should be ready to test your new application. If you have not already done so, save your new Scratch application project and then switch over to Presentation mode and click on the green flag button.

As you work with the Doodle Drawing application, be sure to click on every one of its buttons to make sure the pen switches its color when drawing. Also, experiment with each of the application's line sizes to ensure they are working properly.

Summary

This chapter's focus was on teaching you how to work with Scratch's virtual pen to draw all kinds of different lines, shapes, and graphics. You learned how to enable and disable drawing by controlling the pen's up and down position. You learned how to modify the color and pen width and control the level of shading that is applied. You also learned how to capture a sprite's costume, use it to stamp its image on the stage, and clear off any drawing operations from the stage. Finally, through the development of the Doodle Drawing application, you got to put all of this new information to practical use.

PART III

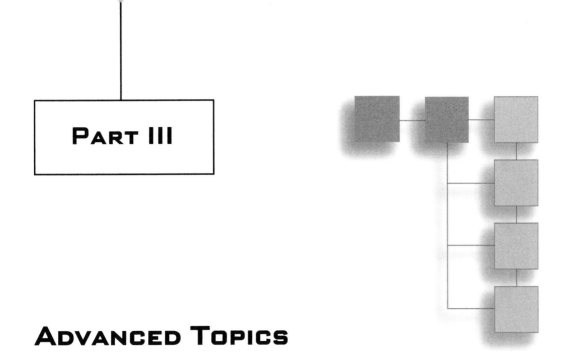

ADVANCED TOPICS

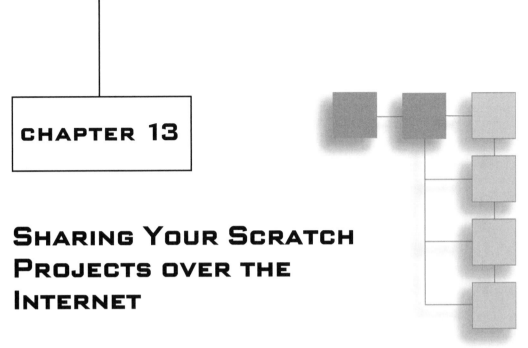

CHAPTER 13

SHARING YOUR SCRATCH PROJECTS OVER THE INTERNET

Scratch's slogan is "Imagine, Program, Share." As the slogan implies, sharing is a big part of Scratch. The Scratch website is specifically designed to facilitate sharing and to promote the development of a large global community of Scratch programmers. By sharing ideas and projects with other Scratch programmers, you not only help others to learn but you increase your own knowledge and experience as well. This chapter will teach you everything you need to know about how to upload, manage, and share your Scratch applications on the Scratch website, helping you to become an active member of Scratch's global community.

The major topics covered in this chapter include learning how to:

- Register a new account at the Scratch website

- Upload your Scratch applications

- Delete applications that you have uploaded

- Post comments and add tags to your uploaded applications

- Create galleries in which you can store and organize your applications

Running Scratch Applications on the Internet

Scratch is all about learning and sharing. The Scratch website (http://scratch.mit.edu) is specifically designed to facilitate both of these objectives, making it easy for you to upload and run your Scratch applications online and

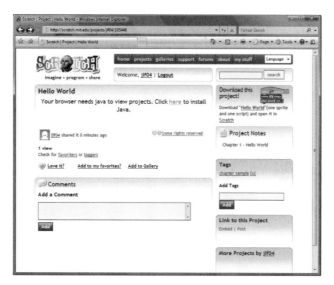

Figure 13.1
Determining if your browser supports Java so that it can run Scratch applications.

to run and download applications submitted by members of the global Scratch community.

Note

At the time this book was written, over 125,000 Scratch projects had already been posted on the Scratch website, providing a wealth of examples that you can download, study, and learn.

To view and run Scratch applications on the Scratch website, you need to use a web browser that supports Java. As an easy way to determine if Java is installed on your browser, visit the Scratch website and click on one of the many available Scratch projects. If the application opens, then Java is installed and working correctly. However, if you see results similar to those shown in Figure 13.1, Java is not installed.

If you determine that you need to install Java, you can do so for free by visiting http://www.java.com/en/download, clicking on the Free Java Download button, and following the instructions that are provided.

Registering with the Scratch Website

In order to upload your Scratch applications to the Scratch website, you must first register for a free Scratch account. To do so, go to http://scratch.mit.edu/signup as shown in Figure 13.2 and fill out the required form.

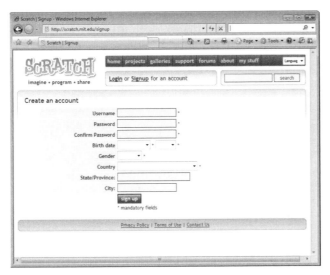

Figure 13.2
You must register with the Scratch website before you can upload your applications.

Figure 13.3
Once registered, you can upload applications and create galleries in which to store your applications.

Note

If you are over 18 years of age, you will also be prompted to supply your email address.

Once you have finished filling out the required information, click on the Sign Up button. A new account will then be created for you, and you will be logged into the website, as demonstrated in Figure 13.3.

Once you have created a new account, you can begin uploading your Scratch applications. At the time this book was written, the Scratch website placed a 10MB limit on the size of application projects that could be uploaded. The purpose of this restriction is to ensure that plenty of space is made available to all members of the Scratch community and to help ensure that upload and download times are kept to a reasonable level.

Once they are uploaded, you can manage your uploaded Scratch applications by logging in to the Scratch website using your new account. There is one important point you need to know: Once uploaded to the Scratch website, there is no way to restrict or keep private any of your Scratch applications. Everything uploaded is made available to anyone who visits the website.

Uploading Your Scratch Applications

The first step in sharing a Scratch application is to click on the Share! button located at the top of the Scratch IDE, displaying the window shown in Figure 13.4. Begin by keying in your account name and password and then provide a name for your project. Next, enter any notes that you think other Scratch programmers visiting the Scratch website will need to know to work with your application.

Figure 13.4
You can provide detailed information about your applications when uploading them.

Note

In addition to providing instructions about how to work with your application, you should also use the Project Notes area to acknowledge the source of any audio or graphic files that you use in your application.

Scratch also supports an optional tagging feature that you can use to help other Scratch programmers locate your applications when searching the Scratch website. By default, Scratch lets you select any of six predefined tags covering the following categories.

- Animation

- Art

- Game

- Music

- Simulation

- Story

In addition, you can also create as many as four custom tags by supplying keywords that you think best describe your application and its purpose. Once you have finished filling out this window, click on the OK button, and the upload process will begin.

Note

Note the option located at the bottom of the Upload to Scratch Server window. This option is automatically selected by default. It instructs Scratch to compress any sound and image files that make up your application before uploading them to the Scratch website. Compressing audio and image files during upload has no effect on the files stored on your computer. This is in direct contrast to the compress sounds and compress images commands provided by the Extras button on the Scratch IDE. These two commands compress any audio and graphic files used in your application.

Once it is compressed, you cannot uncompress a sound or graphic file, so you should plan on maintaining an original copy of your media files someplace for safekeeping. Given the ability to automatically compress sounds and images on the fly when uploading your Scratch applications, there is very little need for the commands provided on the Extras button.

Once an upload is started, a dialog window similar to the one shown in Figure 13.5 is displayed, allowing you to track the progress of the upload process.

Figure 13.5
Scratch keeps you abreast of what is happening as it uploads your applications.

Figure 13.6
You can click on the scratch.mit.edu link to launch your browser and view your uploaded applications.

Figure 13.7
The uploaded application is visible and ready to run online.

One the upload process has completed, the dialog window shown in Figure 13.6 will be displayed.

If you want, you can click on the blue scratch.mit.edu link located in the middle of the dialog window to automatically open your browser and log yourself into the home page of the Scratch website, where you will find your uploaded application waiting on you, as demonstrated in Figure 13.7.

Viewing and Organizing Your Applications Online

Any Scratch application projects that you upload to the Scratch website are stored on your home page on the website, as demonstrated in Figure 13.8.

From here you can run your application, post comments for it, add additional tags, and create galleries into which to organize your applications. You can also delete any projects that you have uploaded and view comments posted by other members of the Scratch community.

Running Your Application

Once they are uploaded, you can view and execute your applications online by clicking on them. This opens the application and makes it ready for execution, as demonstrated in Figure 13.9.

Once it is opened, you can interact with and run your application in exactly the same manner as you did when running it on your local computer. For example, the green flag and red Stop Everything buttons are both clearly visible in the upper-right corner of the online stage. Once they are started, you can interact with Scratch applications using the mouse and keyboard as well.

Adding Comments

You can share additional information about your Scratch application by posting comments. To do so, scroll down the screen as demonstrated in Figure 13.10 to expose the Add a Comment entry field.

Figure 13.8
Once logged onto the Scratch website, you can view, execute, and manage all your applications.

Figure 13.9
Your online application can be run in exactly the same way you run it on your computer.

Figure 13.10
Adding comments to your Scratch application.

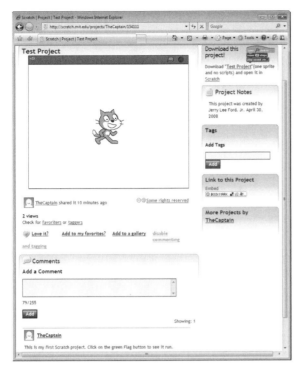

Figure 13.11
Viewing the comments posted about your application.

You can enter any text that you want into this field and then click on the Add button to post your comments. Once posted, your comments, as well as any comments that other members of the Scratch community post about your application, are visible. For example, Figure 13.11 demonstrates how comments look once posted.

As you can see, comments are posted at the bottom of the web page, as is the account name of the individuals who post them.

Adding Tags

In addition to adding tags to your application projects when uploading them, you can also add them online. As demonstrated in Figure 13.12, tags are displayed to the right of your application once it has been opened.

You can add new tags, one at a time, by keying them in to the Add Tags field and then clicking on the Add button. You can also delete any tag that you no longer consider useful by clicking on the [x] characters located just to the right of the tag.

Figure 13.12
Adding tags to your applications makes them easier to find.

Creating Galleries

As you begin to upload your Scratch applications, you may find it helpful to organize them into different galleries. A gallery is a collection of Scratch applications. Typically, most Scratch programmers group their applications into related collections. For example, you may create one gallery to organize your games and a separate gallery for your other applications.

To create a gallery, go to your home page and scroll down and click on the Create link located in the Galleries section on the left-hand side of the web page. This will display the Create New Gallery page, as shown in Figure 13.13.

To create a gallery, you provide it with a name and description, and you specify who can add projects to it. You choices of who can add projects to your gallery include:

- Only Me

- My Friends

- Everyone

You can access your gallery by clicking on its link, which automatically adds a Galleries area to the bottom-left side of the page, as demonstrated in Figure 13.14.

Figure 13.13
Creating a new gallery where you can store your Scratch applications.

Figure 13.14
You can access your new gallery by clicking on the link at the bottom of the web page.

You can add a Scratch application to one of your galleries by opening the application and then clicking on the Add to a Gallery link located just below the stage area. When you do this, the web page expands to include a Where Do You Want to Add section, as demonstrated in Figure 13.15.

Figure 13.15
Adding an application to a gallery.

This section displays a list of all your galleries. To add the application to a gallery, select the check box control to the left of the gallery's name.

You can display a listing of all of the applications stored in your gallery by opening the gallery. For example, the gallery shown in Figure 13.16 currently has a single application stored in it.

In addition to viewing your own gallery, you can browse any gallery on the Scratch website by clicking on the Galleries button located at the top of any Scratch web page. In response, a list of galleries is displayed. By default, 10 galleries are displayed at a time, and you can navigate through the entire list using the navigation controls located on the right-hand side of the page, as demonstrated in Figure 13.17.

The most recently created galleries are displayed first. However, by clicking on the buttons located near the top of the page, you can display galleries based on which ones have the most projects, or you can view featured galleries.

Figure 13.16
Managing your gallery.

Figure 13.17
Exploring application galleries.

Removing Projects

If you decide that you want to remove any of the applications you have uploaded to the Scratch website, you may do so by displaying your list of projects, selecting one or more using the application's check box control (located just underneath it), and then clicking on the Delete Selected Project button, as shown in Figure 13.18.

Updating Your Projects

If after uploading one of your Scratch applications to the Scratch website you decide to make changes to it that you would like to share, you may do so by simply uploading it again, using the exact same name that you used to upload it the first time. If you want to keep the original copy of the application intact on the Scratch website, then you will need to assign a different name to the updated version of your application before you upload it.

Other Scratch Website Features

The Scratch website supports many other features related to the sharing of Scratch application projects that have not been discussed in this chapter but

Figure 13.18
Deleting an application that you have uploaded to the Scratch website.

which you may want to investigate and learn more about. For example, you can change your personal profile information by uploading a picture to represent who you are. You can also change your password. As you browse the website, you can add applications that you really like to a favorites list, making them easy to return to and find again.

You can delete your galleries by clicking on the Delete This Gallery button when viewing one of your galleries. You can add projects that you have uploaded into galleries by opening the gallery that you want to place the application into and then clicking on the Add My Project button. This displays a list of your projects, allowing you to select which ones you want to move into the current gallery. You can even upload a custom graphic from your desktop to be used to represent your gallery.

Downloading Other People's Projects

In addition to allowing you to upload and share your Scratch application projects with Scratch programmers from around the world, the Scratch website also offers access to all of the application projects that other programmers have uploaded. As such, you have instant access to a virtually unlimited number of Scratch applications, all of which you can view, run, and if you want, download. Once it is downloaded, you can study the application and see how it works. If you have ideas for making it better, you can use it as the basis for creating your own version of the application.

Downloading a Scratch application project is easy. First, locate and open the application that you want to download, and then look for its download link, located in the upper-right corner of the web page, as demonstrated in Figure 13.19.

Once you click on a Scratch project's Download link, a File Download window is displayed, asking you what you want to do. Your choices are to open a copy of the application into Scratch on your local computer or to download the application as a file to your computer, allowing to you open and work with it later.

Note

If you elect to open an application project using Scratch, you can still save a copy of it on your computer using Scratch's Save As button. If you elect to download the application project as a file, the file that is downloaded can then be easily identified by its name, the familiar Scratch cat icon, and its .sb file extension.

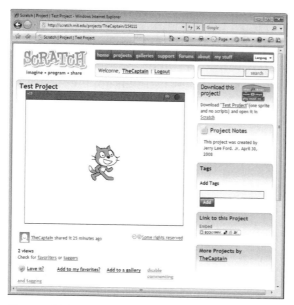

Figure 13.19
Downloading an application from the Scratch website.

Summary

This chapter provided instruction on how to upload your Scratch applications to the Scratch website. Doing so allows you to share your work with other members of the Scratch global community. The Scratch website places thousands of applications at your fingertips, allowing you to not only run them but to download them and see how they work. Through the exchange of application projects, you can become a much more knowledgable and effective programmer, leveraging not only your own work but also the work and ideas of others.

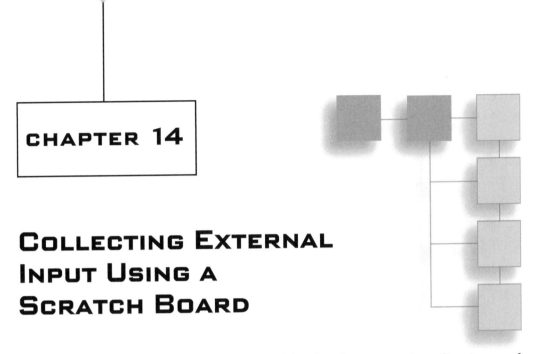

CHAPTER 14

COLLECTING EXTERNAL INPUT USING A SCRATCH BOARD

In addition to using Scratch to develop all kinds of games and applications and interacting with those games and applications using the mouse and keyboard, Scratch is also designed to interact with a special piece of hardware known as a Scratch Board. Using a Scratch Board, you can create applications that are capable of sensing and collecting real-world input. Scratch Boards come with a number of built-in controls, including a slider, a button, and four pairs of alligator clips, as well as two sensors that allow it to capture light and sound data. This chapter will teach you everything you need to know to work with a Scratch Board, including how to install and programmatically interact with it.

The major topics covered in this chapter include:

- Learning how to purchase a Scratch Board

- Downloading and installing Scratch Board software

- Using sensing code blocks to programmatically interact with a Scratch Board

- Keeping an eye on Scratch Board data using different types of monitors

Interacting with the Real World

A Scratch Board is a specialized piece of hardware, shown in Figure 14.1, which you can purchase directly from the Scratch website and attach to your computer via a USB connection. Once a Scratch Board is connected to your computer, your Scratch applications can begin collecting, processing, and responding to different types of real-world data, collected by the Scratch Board's built-in set of sensors and controls.

Scratch Boards come equipped with a number of controls and sensors; their functions are outlined here:

- **Slider.** Detects the current position of the Scratch Board's slider control.

- **Light Sensor.** Detects the amount of light that is currently visible through the Scratch Board's light sensor.

- **Button.** Returns a value of true or false, depending on whether the Scratch Board's button is being pressed.

- **Sound Sensor.** Detects the loudness of sounds through the Scratch Board's sound sensor.

- **Alligator Clips.** Provides a measurement of the electrical resistance in a circuit.

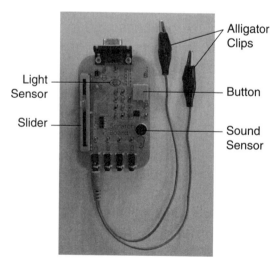

Figure 14.1
Scratch Boards allow your applications to incorporate external input into your applications.

The rest of this chapter is dedicated to teaching you how to install and interact with a Scratch Board. In doing so, you will be able to incorporate a whole new range of input into your applications, using for example variations of light and sound to control the execution.

Tip

In addition to the information provided in this chapter, you can learn more about Scratch Boards by visiting http://scratch.wik.is/Support/Scratch_Board. Among the items you will find on this web page is a link to a small Getting Started with Scratch Boards PDF manual, which provides a number of excellent example scripts that demonstrate how to interact with and use input collected and reported by Scratch Boards.

Buying a Scratch Board

Scratch Boards can only be purchased from the Scratch website. At the time this book was written, the price of a Scratch Board was $25, along with an additional $5 charge for shipping and handling. To verify the current price of a Scratch Board, visit http://scratch.wik.is/Support/Scratch_Board/Pricing_information. To order a Scratch Board, go to https://scratch.media.mit.edu/pages/scratchboard-purchase and fill out the required form.

Installing Your Scratch Board

Installing a Scratch Board on your computer is a relatively quick and easy process and begins with downloading the software driver. Two different types of software driver downloads are available, one for Microsoft Windows and one for Mac OS X. To download the drivers for your computer, go to http://scratch.mit.edu/pages/scratchboardsetup and click on one of the following links (Windows Vista users can skip this step because your computer should automatically install the needed software driver):

- Windows XP (and older) Driver

- Mac OS X Driver

Once you have downloaded the appropriate software driver for your computer, you need to install it. On Microsoft Windows this means extracting the installation program from the Zip file, double-clicking on it, and then following the instructions that are provided.

For Mac OS X users, installing Scratch's software drivers involves opening the file that is downloaded and then double-clicking on the .dmg file that is stored inside. This displays a .pkg program, which when double-clicked executes the driver installation process. Click on Continue to begin the installation process and then follow the instructions that are presented.

Once you have installed the software driver on your computer, connect the USB portion of the cable that came with your Scratch Board to your computer's USB port and then connect the serial portion of the cable to your Scratch Board. At this point your Scratch Board should be ready to use.

Using the Sensor Block to Interact with Your Scratch Board

In order to programmatically interact with a Scratch Board, you need to work with the two sensing code blocks shown in Figure 14.2.

The first code block shown in Figure 14.2 returns a range of data, from 1 to 100, for the selected Scratch Board sensor. In addition, you can select this code block's check box to enable the display of a monitor on the stage, allowing you to keep track of the data that the sensor is returning. This code block works with the slider, light, sound, and all four of the resistance controls (alligator clips).

The second code block shown in Figure 14.2 returns a value of true or false, depending on whether the Scratch Board's button control has been pressed or one of the resistance controls has been used to establish an electrical connection (the alligator clips are connected to one another).

Examples of how to work with both of these sensing code blocks to receive data collected by each of the Scratch Board's sensors and controls are provided throughout the rest of this book.

Collecting Input Using the Slider Control

In order to work with the Scratch Board's slider control, you must use the first sensing code block shown in Figure 14.2. This means dragging and dropping an

Figure 14.2
Access to a Scratch Board is provided through these two sensing code blocks.

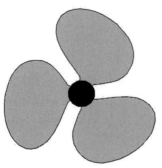

Figure 14.3
The speed at which the fan spins will be controlled by the Scratch Board's slider control.

instance of the code block into another control, where it can be used to provide input; then select Slider from the list of choices displayed in the control's drop-down list.

As an example of how to work with the control, let's create a new Scratch application that emulates a virtual fan. To do this, you will create a new application and then import the sprite shown in Figure 14.3 into it. You will find a copy of this spite on the book's companion CD-ROM. You will also need to remove the default Cat sprite.

Once added to your application, select the sprite and then add the following script to it. As you can see, this script places the sprite representing a fan in the middle of the stage and then uses a loop to retrieve a continuous feed of data from the Scratch Board's slider control. Using this data collected from the Scratch Board as input, a motion block is used to rotate the sprite.

The sprite has been set up so that its rotational center is directly in the center of the black circle in the middle of the sprite. Moving the slider by a small amount will make the fan begin to slowly spin. Moving the slider control by a larger amount will increase the speed at which the fan spins. Using a similar approach, you can use a Scratch Board as an input device for all kinds of Scratch applications. For example, you might use it as a means of controlling a paddle in a Breakout-style game or to control the assignment of data to a variable, which in turn is used to control an application's operation. The possibilities are endless.

Using the Button Control to Initiate Action

In order to work with the Scratch Board's button control, you must use the first sensing code block shown in Figure 14.2. Using this code block, you can determine whether the Scratch Board's button control is being pressed. As an example, let's create another application. Begin by removing the default Cat sprite and then click on the Choose New Sprite from File button, drill down into the Things folder, select the basketball sprite, and click on OK.

Once it is added, select the basketball sprite and add the following script to it:

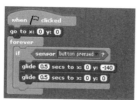

As you can see, this script begins by positioning the sprite at the center of the stage. It then starts a loop to repeatedly execute a conditional code block that checks to see if the Scratch Board's button is being pressed. If this is the case, the statements located inside the condition code block are executed. As a result, the image of the basketball is made to bounce. Figure 14.4 depicts how the basketball looks as it begins its upward bounce.

The basketball will repeatedly bounce for as long as the Scratch Board's button is being pressed and will stop bouncing as soon as the button is released. Using the previous example as a starting point, you should be able to use a Scratch Board's button control as an input device for all kinds of Scratch applications. For example, you might use it in place of the mouse button as a means of controlling when to shoot a missile in a *Space Invaders*-style game.

Reacting to Light

In addition to the slider and button control, you can retrieve input from the light sensor located on your Scratch Board to provide input to your applications. You

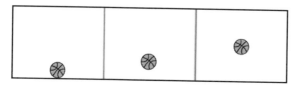

Figure 14.4
Using the Scratch Board's button to control the bouncing of a virtual basketball.

can use either of Scratch's two sensing code blocks to interact with the light sensor. To get a better feel of how to work with the light sensor, let's modify the previous application so that it responds to a change in light in place of the Scratch Board's button control. To do so, modify the application's script as shown here.

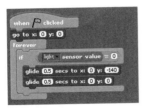

As you can see, the script has been redesigned so that it only bounces the basketball when the Scratch Board's light sensor returns a value of 0 (total darkness). To test out the execution of this script, place your hand over the Scratch Board so that it blocks out the light. When you do, the basketball should start bouncing. Remove your hand so that the Scratch Board can detect some light, and the basketball will stop bouncing.

Using this example as a starting point, you could create a Scratch application that performs a certain task only when the lights have been turned off or on. You might also use your Scratch Board as the basis for creating an alarm clock that awakens you when the sun comes up.

Responding to Sound

In addition to providing your application with data based on the amount of light it is able to detect, your Scratch Board can also detect variations in the loudness of sounds. For example, you could easily modify the script belonging to the application that you have been experimenting with to work with sound in place of light.

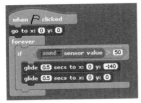

As redesigned, the script will now bounce the basketball only when the Scratch Board detects a relatively loud noise in the room. The sound sensor returns a range of numbers from 1 to 100, where 0 represents total silence, and 100 represents maximum volume. To see how this change affects your application, start your application and make a little noise. If the basketball does not move, make another noise, this time a little louder. Keep going until you make a noise that is loud enough to trigger the bouncing of the basketball.

Note

The sensing code block shown in the preceding example operates much like the sensing code block shown here.

Unlike this code block, which reports on the loudness of the computer's microphone, the sensing code block used in the example retrieves its data directly from the Scratch Board's microphone.

Using sound as a trigger for script execution, you could, for example, create and execute an application that plays an alarm whenever it detects someone in your room, warning him that his presence has been detected, thus creating your own virtual watch dog.

Measuring Electrical Resistance

In addition to working with the Scratch Board's slider, button, light sensor, and sound sensor, the Scratch Board also comes equipped with four sets of alligator clips, which you can attach to the bottom of the Scratch Board. Each set of alligator clips represents an individual sensor, which you can use to provide your applications with input based on the strength of the electrical resistance in any circuit you set up.

As an example of how you might work with an alligator clip, let's modify the script for the application that you have been experimenting with, as shown here:

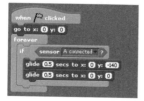

With this modified script now in place, you must touch both ends of the alligator clips together in order to make the basketball bounce. To test how well different materials conduct electricity, you could attach both ends of the alligator clips to different objects to see if enough current passes through to make the basketball bounce. With access to four separate sets of alligator clips, you can create all sorts of different tests and even run them all at once.

Keeping a Watchful Eye on Sensor Data

Scratch allows you to display individual monitors for each of the different types of sensor controls supported by either of the two sensing code blocks that work with the Scratch Board. To do so, click on the Sensing button located at the top of the blocks palette, then click on the drop-down list located in the sensing code block you plan on working with and select the sensor that you want to keep an eye on. Next, select the check box located just to the left of the code block. A monitor for the selected Scratch Board sensor will then appear on the stage. If you want to display additional monitors, you may do so by selecting the code block's drop-down list again to select a different sensor. You will have to select the block's check box again. Using this approach, you can display a monitor for as many of the Scratch Board's sensors as you want, as demonstrated in Figure 14.5.

To disable the display of any monitor that you enable, you must perform the procedure outlined above in reverse order to clear out the check box for each sensor. A quicker and easier way of keeping an eye on the data being supplied by multiple sensors is to enable the display of the Scratch Board Watcher, as shown in Figure 14.6.

To enable the display of the Scratch Board Watcher, right-click on the sensing code block that you plan to use and select Show Scratch Board Watcher from the

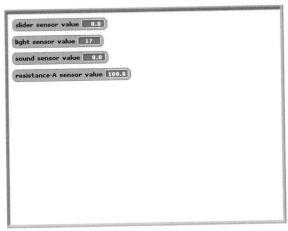

Figure 14.5
Displaying individual monitors to report on different Scratch Board sensors.

Figure 14.6
The Scratch Board Watcher lets you keep track of all of the data being supplied by your Scratch Board.

popup menu that is displayed. When you are done with the Scratch Board Watcher, you can remove it from the stage by right-clicking on it and selecting Hide from the popup menu.

Summary

In this chapter, you learned all about Scratch Boards. This included learning how to purchase and install them. You learned how to programmatically interact with them using sensing code blocks and saw examples of how to work with all of the Scratch Board's controls and sensors. These examples included the creation of scripts that can react to changes in light and sound level as well as to button presses, slider bar movement, and changes in electrical current. This chapter also demonstrated how to work with different monitors that allow you to keep track of the data being collected and reported by your Scratch Board.

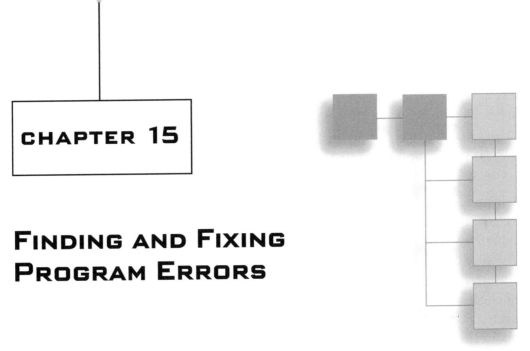

CHAPTER 15

FINDING AND FIXING PROGRAM ERRORS

Compared to most programming languages, Scratch is less prone to many types of programming errors, often referred to as bugs. As a programmer, your job is to seek out and remove all of the programming bugs from your applications and to ensure that they operate as they are supposed to. That's where this chapter comes in. By the time you are done reading it, you will have a solid understanding of the types of errors that Scratch is susceptible to and the basic steps involved in tracking down and fixing them. In addition, you will learn about different resources that you can turn to in order to get help.

The major topics covered in this chapter include:

- Understanding the differences between syntax, logical, and run-time errors
- Learning how to run applications in single stepping mode
- Accessing code block help
- Getting help from the Scratch global community

Dealing with Application Errors

Program errors, sometimes referred to as bugs, are a programmer's number one problem. Errors can occur for a number of different reasons and can cause your applications to misbehave or even prevent them from executing at all. As your projects inevitably get larger and more complex, the possibility and frequency of errors also increase. That's just the way it is.

The goal of this chapter is to help you gain an understanding of the different types of errors that you will run into and provide you with guidance on how to go about locating and eliminating them from your applications. Some errors are easy to find, especially in small scripts, while others can be quite challenging to locate and often can only be found through intense testing and debugging.

Fortunately, there are steps that you can take to reduce the number of errors that occur in your applications. For starters, take a little extra time to plan out the design of your applications rather than making things up as you go along. Another important step is to create your application scripts a few code blocks at a time, frequently testing as you go along, rather than waiting until your entire application has been built to see how things work. In addition, you should set aside a little extra time at the end of the development process just for testing your applications and making sure that they not only meet your expectations but do so without generating any errors.

In addition to the programming practices discussed above, there are a number of other steps that you can take to make sure your Scratch applications work like you want them to. These steps include:

- Taking a little extra time to carefully design and lay out your application's interface

- Ensuring that you provide clear instructions on how to properly work with your application

- Creating descriptive names for all application variables

- Renaming all the sprites, sounds, and costumes used in your application to make them more intuitive to work with

- Breaking down programming logic into a number of manageable small scripts as opposed to a few really large ones

Unfortunately, no matter how much you try, you can never totally avoid all of the different types of errors that Scratch applications are susceptible to. Broadly speaking, most programming languages are susceptible to the following types of errors:

- Syntax errors

- Logical errors

- Run-time errors

Each of these three types of errors is discussed in the sections that follow.

Understanding Syntax Errors

One of the things that makes Scratch unique among programming languages is the way it prevents syntax errors. A *syntax error* is an error that occurs when a programmer fails to write code statements in a manner that follows the syntax rules specified by the programming language. Scratch code blocks are designed to fit together in logical ways like pieces in a puzzle. Scratch only allows you to snap together blocks in ways that make syntactic sense. As a result, Scratch eliminates syntax errors that proliferate in other programming languages.

Keeping an Eye Out for Logical Errors

One category of errors you need to worry about regardless of the programming language you are working with is logical errors. A *logical error* is an error that occurs because of a mistake on your part in the implementation of the programming logic you applied to solving a problem or performing task. For example, suppose you had an application that needed to add two numbers together, but when you assembled the programming logic you accidentally subtracted one number from another. As a result, your application will not run correctly. From Scratch's perspective, everything would be fine, since there was technically no problem with the logic you implemented. As soon as you see that the results tallied by the application are not correct, you should immediately suspect that you have a logical error to debug.

As another example of a logical error, consider the following pair of scripts, which belong to an application that uses the default Cat sprite to display text messages that are supposed to count from 1 to 5.

Both scripts begin their execution when the green flag button is clicked. When this happens, the first script assigns a starting value of 0 to a variable named Counter and then goes into a loop that has been set up to wait until the value of Counter is equal to 5. When this occurs, the sprite is made to display a message, and then all script activity within the sprite is halted.

The second script is responsible for making the sprite count from 1 to 5, incrementing the value of Counter each time the sprite says a number. If you were to run this example, you would see that as it is currently written, it has a logical error. Specifically, the second script loop was accidentally set up to run four times instead of five times. As a result, the sprite only counts from 1 to 4, and since the value of Counter never reaches 5, the first script gets stuck in its loop. Only by fixing the loop in the second script (so that it executes five times) can this logical error be fixed.

The best way to identify logical errors is to take a little extra time to carefully plan out the design of your applications and to test them extensively, ensuring that they run exactly as you expect them to. If, despite your best efforts, a logical error manages to make its way into your program logic, all hope is not lost. Using the debugging techniques discussed later in this chapter, you should be able to track down and eliminate all of the errors from your Scratch applications.

Tracking Down Run-Time Errors

A third category of errors that plagues all programming languages, including Scratch, is run-time errors. A *run-time error* is an error that occurs when a Scratch script attempts to perform an illegal action. Scratch automatically identifies run-time errors when they occur by surrounding the script where the error occurred with a red outline. Depending on how your applications are designed, it is entirely possible that you might be able to run them over and over again without ever executing the script in the application where a run-time error lies. This is why it is so important that you thoroughly test the execution of every script in your applications. Failure to do so leaves you open to run-time errors.

As an example of what a run-time error looks like when reported by Scratch, take a look at the following script.

Here, Scratch has flagged the script as having a run-time error. The reason for the error resides in the `Variable` code block. As you can see, it includes an embedded `Numbers` block that attempts to divide 10 by 0. However, the division of 10 by 0 is an illegal action in all modern programming languages, including Scratch.

The unfortunate thing about run-time errors is that if you do not identify and eliminate them during application development, you can bet that your users will find them for you, which is the last thing any programmer wants to happen.

Debugging Your Scratch Applications

No matter how carefully you plan out your Scratch scripts, somewhere along the line you are going to run into errors. As previously demonstrated, Scratch helps you locate and identify scripts that contain run-time errors, and while your Scratch applications are not subject to syntax errors, logical errors can be particularly difficult to track down and identify. Fortunately, there are a number of debugging techniques that you can employ to help you track down and eliminate problems within your application's scripts.

Basic Debugging Techniques

One of the challenges in debugging a Scratch application is to identify when things are happening. Scratch helps simplify this challenge a bit by highlighting scripts when they execute. However, the exact activity occurring within a given script can be hard to identify. This makes it difficult to determine if things are occurring in both the order and manner that you intend for them to.

Making a Little Noise

Once way of figuring out what is happening within an application is to embed code blocks inside your scripts for the purpose of notifying you when things occur. For example, using a sound block you could play a note every time a particular variable is updated during the execution of your script. Using this sound as a means of keeping track of updates, you could verify that a variable's value is being properly set when testing the application. If during testing you do not hear the sound played, then you know that something is wrong. If the variable that you are watching is modified in more than one place within a script, or if it can be modified by different scripts, you might want to play different notes at each location where variable modifications occur. Then by simply keeping your ears open when testing the execution of your application, you may be able to track down the script or area where the problem lies.

Display Informative Messages

Of course, you do not have to work with sound blocks. If you prefer to, you can work with looks blocks instead. Looks blocks provide the added benefit of being able to display text, which you can use as marker within script execution to let you identify exactly when certain parts of a script are executing. For example, you might begin each script with a looks block that displays a text message announcing that the script is executing and end each script by displaying a closing message. You might embed additional looks blocks at key locations within your script to notify when specific things happen. If, for example, when testing an application, a particular text message is not displayed when you expect it to be, then you will know where to begin looking for the source of the problem.

Tip

If you think that a variable is not being set correctly during script execution, you can enable the display of a monitor so that you can keep your eye on the variable's assigned value when testing your application. However, if your application utilizes a larger number of variables, displaying lots of monitors can get in the way of things. As an alternative, you can keep an eye on the value of a variable by displaying it inside a looks blocks, as demonstrated in Figure 15.1.

Figure 15.1
Using a looks block to report on a variable's assigned value.

Although not obvious because of the shape of some looks blocks' input fields, you can use them as shown above to display a variable's value.

Slowing Things Down

Because of the speed at which things tend to happen in many applications, it can be difficult to keep track of what is going on. If you are using looks blocks to display helpful text messages, you can slow things down by pausing script execution for a specified number of seconds. Alternatively, you can also slow things down by using the control block shown in Figure 15.2 to pause script execution.

By temporarily halting a script, you can give yourself time to check on variable values to see if they have been correctly set and poke around and look at the

Figure 15.2
You can use this code block to slow down script execution.

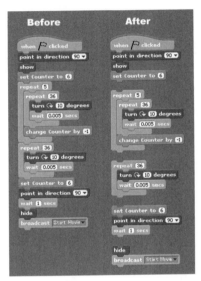

Figure 15.3
Testing a script by breaking it down into smaller parts.

activity of other scripts. This is especially helpful in applications made up of multiple scripts and scripts where broadcast messages and variables are used to coordinate the execution of script activity.

Testing Individual Scripts

When testing your Scratch applications, it is important that you make sure that every script gets executed. Otherwise, you may miss out on finding a potential problem. To make sure this happens, take time to test all of the functionality and features of your applications. One easy way to do this is to double-click on every script in your application and observe the effects of its execution.

Breaking Things Down into Smaller Pieces

Really large scripts can be challenging to test because of their size and inherent complexity. One easy way of getting around this challenge is to break these scripts down into smaller parts when individually testing them. As an example of how you might do this, take a look at Figure 15.3.

By breaking down a script like the one in Figure 15.3 into multiple parts, you can double-click on each part and examine its effects on your application. Should something unexpected occur, you will know exactly which part of your script to focus on to find the source of an application's problem.

Making Liberal Use of Monitors

Another important source of information at your disposal that you can use when debugging your application is code block monitors. By temporarily enabling the display of monitors when testing your applications, you can keep track of key data used by your applications. Once you are done testing, you can disable the display of any monitors that you do not need to display as part of the normal operation of the application.

Running Your Application in Single Stepping Mode

In addition to all of the debugging techniques discussed above, Scratch provides one additional debugging tool, known as *single stepping*. When you run an application using single stepping mode, Scratch slows down the speed at which your application executes, making it easier for you to monitor execution flow.

Normally the Scratch IDE highlights an entire script with a white outline when it executes. But when run in single stepping mode, Scratch also highlights individual code blocks as they execute. As your applications execute in single stepping mode, you can monitor their execution flow to determine if things are executing in the proper order.

Note

You can control the speed at which your application executes by pressing the Shift key and left-clicking on the Extras button, then clicking on Set Single Stepping from the popup menu that appears. This displays a list of options to control single stepping execution speed. These choices include:

- Turbo Speed

- Normal

- Flash blocks (fast)

- Flash blocks (slow)

To develop a better understanding of how single stepping works, consider the following series of examples, which demonstrate what you can expect to see when running an application in single stepping mode.

To turn on single stepping mode, click on the Extras button located at the top of the IDE and then click on the Start Single Stepping option from the popup menu that appears. Once single stepping has been enabled, go ahead and start running your application. As the application executes, two things become immediately obvious: Things are occurring more slowly, and in addition to highlighting each script with a white outline as it executes, Scratch now highlights individual code blocks as they execute.

Below is an example of a script that has begun executing, as indicated by the white outline that surrounds the script. Within the script, you can see that the second code block is the code block that is currently executing because Scratch has highlighted it using a yellow color.

Normally, Scratch runs scripts so quickly that it would not be practical to try to monitor the execution of individual code blocks. However, single stepping slows things down enough to let you do so. For example, as shown below, you can clearly see that the fourth code block is now being executed. If you have a monitor for the Counter variable displayed on the stage, you would be able to confirm that the code block has correctly modified the variable value.

Within a few moments, the script enters into a loop and begins the repeated execution of two code blocks. Below you can see how the script looks when the first of these two code blocks is executed. As you can see, this code block rotates its sprite by 10 degrees. You should be able to observe this movement by watching the sprite on the stage.

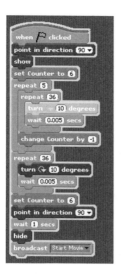

After a brief pause, the second of the two code blocks in the loop executes, as shown here.

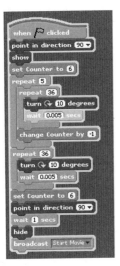

Scratch continues to highlight code blocks one at a time for as long as the script executes, giving you the opportunity to validate that the script is executing exactly as you expect it to and that variables are being modified as you want. If while monitoring script activity you see something happen that you do not expect, you can halt application execution, knowing exactly where the problem lies.

As your application executes in single stepping mode, you can also keep an eye on variable values, ensuring that they are being properly set and modified as you expect them to. You can also switch between sprites and observe other scripts, which will also be executing in single stepping mode.

Hint

Although single stepping is a very helpful debugging tool, it lacks many of the features that are usually included in debugging tools provided by most modern programming languages. For example, it lacks the ability to set breakpoints, which pause execution when certain code statements are reached, giving programmers the ability to access an application's status before allowing the application to continue its execution. Still, single stepping serves its purpose well, and when combined with the debugging techniques covered in this chapter, it should be more than sufficient to help you track and fix any application bug.

Watch Out when Removing Sounds and Sprites

Unlike many programming languages, Scratch is extremely forgiving when it comes to what in many programming languages would be considered a major error. For example, let's say you created a script that played an audio file named meow, as demonstrated below, and you later decided to remove the audio file from your application but forgot to remove the sound block in the script. It would certainly be logical to expect that when you ran your application, an error would occur. But this will not be the case.

Rather than preventing application execution and highlighting the error, Scratch overlooks the problem and runs your application anyway. When it comes time to play the missing audio file, scratch just ignores the problem. This behavior can be a double-edged sword, because on the one hand your application still runs. However, unless you carefully test the execution of your application after deleting the sound file, you may not discover the error, and the overall quality of your application will suffer.

Scratch is just as forgiving when it comes to the management of sprite costumes. Suppose, for example, that you added a costume named bat1-a to a sprite and then used the following script to switch its costume:

If sometime down the road you decided to modify your application by removing the costume from the sprite, Scratch would not flag the oversight as an error and would instead allow your application to run, ignoring the costume switch error when it came across it. Again, this type of behavior is a double-edged sword and can only be overcome by careful modification and retesting of your Scratch applications any time you decide to change or remove a sound, costume, or background.

Getting Help

The development of good debugging skills is an absolute requirement for any serious programmer. However, no matter how good you may be at debugging, there are going to be times when you may need additional help in finding the answer to a particular problem or challenge. Fortunately, there are a number of resources that you can turn to for assistance, both within Scratch and online, as discussed in the following sections.

Referring to Scratch's Online Help

One source of help that you can turn to with the click of a button is the Scratch Help web page, which you can access by clicking on the Want Help? button located at the top of the Scratch IDE. When clicked, Scratch opens your default browser and loads the web page shown in Figure 15.4.

On this web page you will find links to a number of helpful resources, including links that let you open Scratch's Getting Started and Reference Guide PDF manuals as well as its support page. The support page contains additional links to online videos, Scratch Cards, and other information. Also available on the web page is a link labeled Help Screens, which when clicked displays a listing of help screens, as shown in Figure 15.5, each of which is designed to teach you how to work with an individual Scratch code block.

The help screens are organized by category. Using links provides at the top of the web page, you can jump to specific categories of help screens.

Getting Help for Individual Code Blocks

An even faster way of accessing Scratch help screens is to view them one at a time on an as-needed basis without having to go through the Internet to view

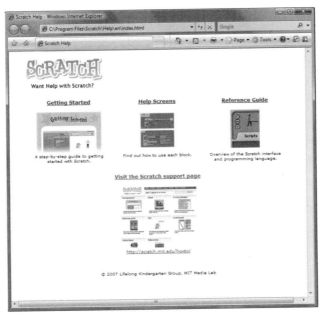

Figure 15.4
Online help is just a single click away.

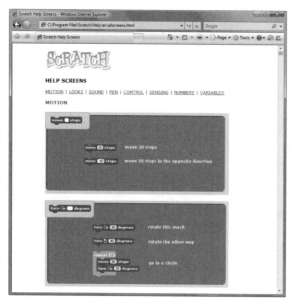

Figure 15.5
Using the Help Screen links, you can quickly view help information for all of Scratch's code blocks.

Figure 15.6
An example of a typical help screen.

them. To view the help screen for an individual code block, right-click on the code block and then click on the help option that appears in the resulting popup menu. For example, Figure 15.6 shows the help screen for one of the sensing blocks.

In this particular example, the help screen demonstrates the code block's usage and provides an example that further demonstrates the effect of using the code block. In addition, more information is provided at the bottom of the help screen that shows all of the code block's available options.

Getting Help from Other Scratch Programmers

In addition to the documentation made available to you through Scratch's help screens, the Scratch website also sponsors a collection of forums that bring together Scratch programmers from around the world. These forums facilitate the free exchange of ideas and provide you with the opportunity to seek out help and advice from fellow Scratch programmers. As shown in Figure 15.7, you can access these forums by going to http://scratch.mit.edu/forums.

Tip

If all else fails and you simply cannot find an answer to a particular problem, you can try sending an email to the Scratch developers by going to http://scratch.mit.edu/contact/us and filling in the email form that is provided. When doing so, provide as much information as possible about your problem and the steps that you have taken in trying to fix it.

Figure 15.7
The forums are organized into a number of high-level categories, including a forum dedicated to discussing troubleshooting.

Figure 15.8
Scratch forums provide the ability to interact with and learn from other Scratch programmers.

By posting your questions to the appropriate forum, you can tap into the expertise and experience of other Scratch programmers. Often, you can find an answer to your problem without having to post a question at all. Answers can often be found in threads already posted by other Scratch programmers. Figure 15.8 shows an example of types of discussions you will find when you visit the Scratch website's forums.

Summary

This chapter taught you about the different types of errors to which Scratch applications are susceptible and examined a number of different ways in which pesky application bugs can be tracked down and eliminated. This included learning how to run your application in stepping mode so that you can monitor the execution of the logical flow within your application while also keeping a watchful eye on variable values. You also learned how to access help from different sources, including the forums sponsored on the Scratch website, where you can receive help from Scratch programmers around the world.

PART IV

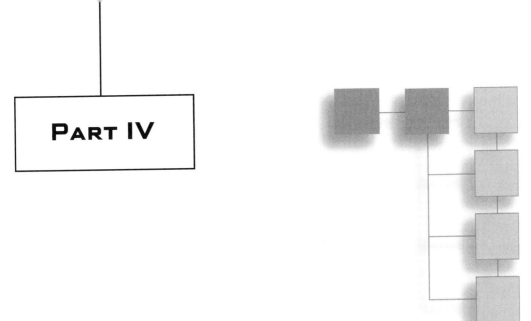

APPENDICES

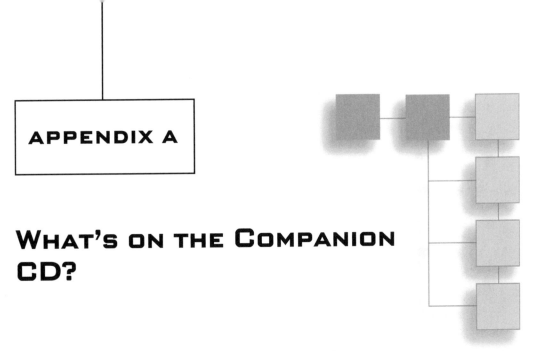

APPENDIX A

What's on the Companion CD?

As you continue to learn more about Scratch and improve your programming skills, it helps to have access to a good collection of source code that you can reference. This book has provided you with numerous sample Scratch application projects. By studying these projects, you can learn a lot about how to program. You can also use this book to find working examples of how to perform different types of tasks and use them as the basis for creating new Scratch application projects. This will not only save you time, but it will also keep you from having to re-invent the wheel and let you keep your focus on tackling new programming challenges.

If you have been faithfully re-creating all of the Scratch application projects presented in this book, then you already have access to such a collection of sample projects. However, if you skipped around a bit, then you may have missed a few sample projects. You will be happy to know that all of the sample Scratch projects covered in this book are available at your fingertips on this book's companion CD.

Scratch Project Source Code

You will find copies of the source file for all of the Scratch projects developed in this book on the companion CD. You will also find copies of any custom graphics and audio files required to build projects. Table A.1 provides a complete list of each of the Scratch project source code files that you will find on the CD.

Table A.1 Scratch Projects Available on the Companion CD

Chapter	File Name
Chapter 1	Hello World.sb
Chapter 4	My. Wiggly's Dance.sb
Chapter 5	Fish Tank.sb
Chapter 6	Family Scrapbook.sb
Chapter 7	Basketball Quiz.sb
Chapter 8	NumberGuess.sb
Chapter 9	Ball Chase.sb
Chapter 10	Crazy Eight Ball.sb
Chapter 11	Family Picture Movie.sb
Chapter 12	Doodle.sb

You will also find each of these projects published on the Scratch website at http://scratch.mit.edu/ in the *Scratch Programming for Teens* gallery.

Note

In addition to all of the sample applications listed in Table A.1, you will also find a bonus application named Scratch Pong on the book's CD-ROM. You will not find this application on the *Scratch Programming for Teens* gallery at the Scratch website.

Scratch Installation Files for Microsoft Windows and Mac OS X

In addition to all of this book's sample projects, you will also find the installation files needed to install Scratch version 1.2.1 on either Microsoft Windows or Mac OS X on the book's companion CD-ROM.

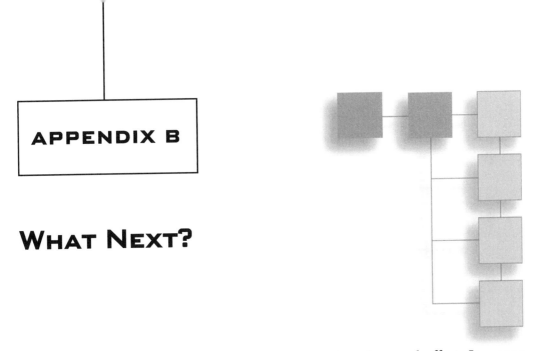

APPENDIX B

WHAT NEXT?

Learning how to become a good programmer takes time and effort. It means putting in the hours necessary to learn the fundamental techniques involved in developing computer application projects. Scratch provides an excellent platform for getting started. It provides a friendly and fun environment in which to learn. A good understanding of Scratch programming will prepare you to make the jump to other programming languages like Visual Basic, AppleScript, C++, and so on.

Learning Scratch requires commitment. By making your way through to the end of this book, you have demonstrated this commitment. Although this book has certainly taught you a lot about Scratch and programming in general, there is still much more to be learned.

To become a world-class programmer, you need to continue your programming education. You need to continue to experiment and learn as much as you can about Scratch. Do not think of this book as the end of your Scratch programming education. Instead, think of it as the beginning. Over the coming weeks and months, you should continue developing new Scratch projects. You should also keep an eye on the different forums hosted on the Scratch website to learn from the experiences of others. Better yet, consider becoming an active member of the Scratch community.

To help you further your understanding of Scratch and to become a better programmer, this appendix provides a list of websites and supplemental reading materials that you can turn to as you continue to develop and hone your programming skills.

Locating Scratch Resources Online

As you would expect, there is an awful lot of helpful information on the Internet about Scratch. By frequenting the websites discussed in the sections that follow, you can keep abreast of the latest happenings in the Scratch community while also keeping your Scratch programming knowledge and skills up to date.

The Scratch Website

The most informative and helpful Scratch website is the Scratch site developed and maintained by MIT located at http://scratch.mit.edu, as shown in Figure B.1.

This site is packed with helpful information, including documentation, video tutorials, and forums where you can go to interact with and learn from other Scratch programmers from around the world. Best of all, this site provides instant access to tons of Scratch projects, all of which you can download, experiment with, and learn from.

Figure B.1
The official home page of the Scratch programming language.

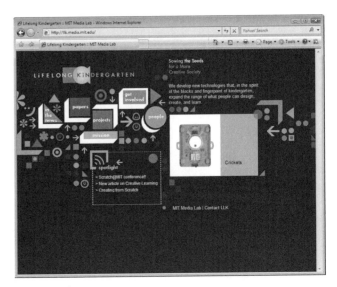

Figure B.2
Scratch is developed by the Lifelong Kindergarten Group at MIT.

The Lifelong Kindergarten Website

Another website that is certainly worth visiting is the Lifelong Kindergarten MIT Media Lab site located at http://llk.media.mit.edu/, as shown in Figure B.2.

This site includes information about Scratch, including links to various papers about Scratch.

The Wikipedia Scratch Page

Another excellent source of Scratch information is the Wikipedia Scratch page located at http://en.wikipedia.org/wiki/Scratch_%28programming_language%29, as shown in Figure B.3.

Here you can find information on Scratch, its origins and creator, as well as its development environment and website. In addition, you will also find plenty of links to papers about Scratch.

The Programming Page at the Thornburg Center Website

If your operating system of choice is Linux, you will be pleased to know that an official Linux version of Scratch is in the works. In the meantime, if you cannot wait, you can download a free user implementation of Scratch at http://tcpdpodcast.org/scratch.html, as shown in Figure B.4.

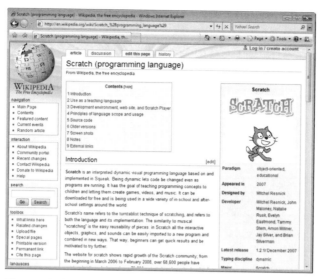

Figure B.3
The Scratch page located at www.wikipedia.org.

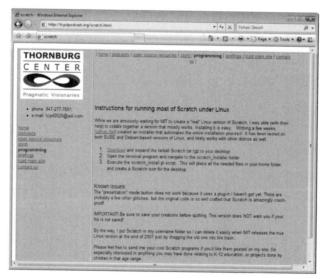

Figure B.4
Downloading a free copy of Scratch for Linux.

You will find all of the instructions you need to download and install Scratch on Linux at this site. Although it does not support Scratch's Presentation mode, this Scratch implementation provides most of the programming features currently available in the Windows and Mac OS X versions of Scratch.

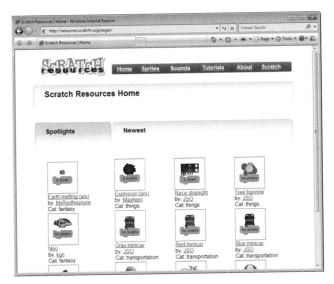

Figure B.5
You can download free sprite and sound files from the Scratch Resources website.

The Scratch Resources Website

Another useful website dedicated to Scratch is the Scratch Resources website located at http://resources.scratchr.org/pages/, as shown in Figure B.5.

This sites provides free access to a growing collection of sprite and sound files, which you are invited to download for free, provided you reference the Scratch Resources website in your Scratch project's credits. In addition to sprite and sound files, you will also find video tutorials designed to help you learn more about programming with Scratch.

Recommended Reading

In addition to the websites previously discussed, you can learn a lot about Scratch by reviewing documentation available on the web. This documentation is available electronically. A brief description of some particularly useful documents, including their locations, is listed here.

- **Getting Started with Scratch.** This 14-page PDF file provides a step-by-step guide to Scratch, demonstrating its basic operation and many of its capabilities. This document can be downloaded from the Support page at the Scratch website (http://scratch.wik.is/Support).

- **Scratch Reference Guide.** This 17-page PDF file provides detailed information about the Scratch graphical interface, its Paint Editor program, and a detailed overview of each of the Scratch blocks. This document can be downloaded from the Support page at the Scratch website (http://scratch.wik.is/Support).

- **Getting Started with Scratch Boards.** This nine-page PDF file provides an overview of Scratch Boards and detailed explanations of how to work with its many different features. It also provides troubleshooting advice. This document can be downloaded from the Scratch Board page at the Scratch website (http://scratch.wik.is/Support/Scratch_Board).

- **An Introduction to Scratch.** This online book is available as a Wikibook through www.wikipedia.org. At the time of writing, the Wikibook was still a work in progress. However, it was already well underway and contained a growing collection of programming information about Scratch. This document can be read online at Wikibooks by visiting http://en.wikibooks.org/wiki/Scratch/Lessons.

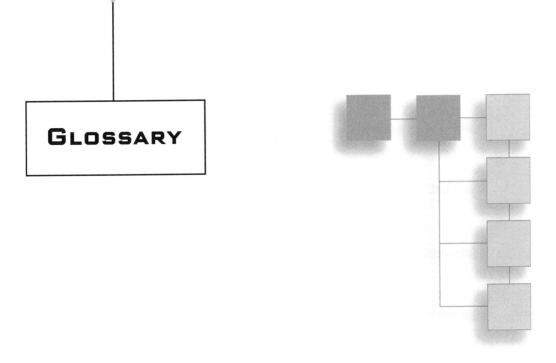

GLOSSARY

Actor. A term used to refer to sprites and the role they play as they interact with one another on the stage.

Animated GIF. A graphic is made up of two or more frames, each of which is displayed as an automated sequence when the GIF file is displayed.

Boolean. A term used to represent data that has either of two values, true or false.

Brightness. The application or restriction of the intensity of light in a graphic image.

Broadcast Message. An electronic message sent between sprites as a means of coordinating application activity.

Code Block. A graphical command used in the creation of a script.

Collision. An event that occurs whenever two sprites come into contact with one another on the stage.

Compression. The process of reducing the size of sound and graphics files in order to reduce the overall size of Scratch applications.

Conditional Logic. The process of executing sets of code blocks based on whether or not a tested condition proves true.

Costumes. Images that are used to represent a sprite on the stage.

Data. A piece of information collected, stored, modified, and processed during application execution.

Debugger. A program or utility that can be used to execute an application within a special environment that allows programmers to slow and monitor the execution of an application's script as it runs.

Decimal. A floating point or real number.

Endless Loop. A loop that does not have a means for terminating its execution.

Event Handling. The process of initiating script execution based on the occurrence of predefined events, such as a mouse click, the pressing of a keyboard key, or the clicking of a sprite.

Fisheye. A graphic effect that can be applied to a sprite or background in order to magnify a portion of its image.

Ghost. A graphic effect that fades the appearance of a costume or background, making it look transparent.

Global Variable. A variable that can be modified by any script in an application.

Gradient. A color created by blending together the foreground and background colors.

Hat Block. A code block that creates event-driven scripts.

IDE (Integrated Development Environment). A graphical application development environment designed to facilitate program development.

Integer. An absolute or whole number that does not have a decimal point.

Java. A popular web-based programming language that is a prerequisite for executing a Scratch application on the Scratch website.

Local Variable. A variable that can be modified only by scripts belonging to the sprite in which the variable is defined.

Logical Error. An error created by a mistake made by the programmer when developing the logic implemented by a script.

Looks Blocks. Code blocks that affect sprite and background appearance and display text.

Loop. A collection of one or more code blocks that are repeatedly executed.

Monitor. A small block that displays the value currently assigned to the code block.

Mosaic. A special graphic effect that creates an image made up of repeated instances of a sprite or background.

Motion Blocks. Code blocks that control sprite placement, direction, rotation, and movement.

MP3. An audio file that utilizes advanced compression technology while retaining high audio quality.

Nest. The process of embedding one set of code blocks within another set of code blocks.

Numbers Blocks. Code blocks that perform mathematical operations, logical comparisons, rounding, and other arithmetic operations.

Order of Precedence. The set of rules that is followed when evaluating a numeric expression.

Paint Editor. A Scratch program that supports the creation of graphics files to be used as the basis for creating and modifying sprites and backgrounds.

Pen. A virtualized drawing tool that can be used to draw on the stage.

Pen Blocks. Code blocks that can be used to draw using different colors and pen sizes.

Pixelate. A special graphic effect that displays a sprite or background at a lower resolution than the resolution at which it was created.

Project. A collection of sprites, scripts, backgrounds, and sounds that is used as the basis for creating Scratch applications.

Real Number. A number that includes a decimal number.

Reporter Block. A code block that has either rounded or angled sides and is specifically designed as a mechanism for providing input for other code blocks to process.

Rotation Center. The point on a sprite that remains in position when a sprite is rotated.

Run-time Error. An application error that occurs when an application attempts to perform an illegal action.

Scope. A term that refers to the area within an application where a variable's value can be accessed and modified.

Scratch Board. A special piece of hardware that you can buy from the Scratch website and attach to your computer in order to collect and process environmental and user-provided input.

Scratch Cards. PDF files that you can print and use as a quick reference for performing certain tasks.

Script. A collection of code blocks that outlines the programming logic that influences the operation of a sprite.

Sensing Blocks. Code blocks that can be used to determine the location of the mouse-pointer, its distance from other sprites, and whether a sprite is touching another sprite.

Sound Blocks. Code blocks that control the playback and volume of musical notes and audio files.

Sprite. A two-dimensional image drawn on a transparent background that can be moved around the stage. You can change its appearance using different costumes.

Squeak. A cross-platform programming language used to develop Scratch.

Stack Blocks. Code blocks with a notch at the top or a bump at the bottom that can be snapped together with other bocks to define a script's programming logic.

Stacks. Another term for a script.

Stage. The background area on the Scratch IDE upon which sprites are displayed during application execution.

String. A set of characters that can be displayed within thought and speech bubbles.

Tempo. A measurement of the speed, in beats per minute, at which a drum or note is played.

Troubleshooting. The identification, location, and elimination of programming errors, or bugs, that prevent applications from executing properly.

Variable. A location in memory where an individual piece of data is stored.

Variable Scope. Identifies the location within an application where the variable's value can be modified.

Variables Blocks. Code blocks that can be used to store data used by applications when they execute.

Wave. A file with a .wav extension that supports the storage and playback of audio files.

Whirl. A special graphic effect that twists and distorts a portion of a costume or background.

INDEX

License Agreement/Notice of Limited Warranty

By opening the sealed disc container in this book, you agree to the following terms and conditions. If, upon reading the following license agreement and notice of limited warranty, you cannot agree to the terms and conditions set forth, return the unused book with unopened disc to the place where you purchased it for a refund.

License

The enclosed software is copyrighted by the copyright holder(s) indicated on the software disc. You are licensed to copy the software onto a single computer for use by a single user and to a backup disc. You may not reproduce, make copies, or distribute copies or rent or lease the software in whole or in part, except with written permission of the copyright holder(s). You may transfer the enclosed disc only together with this license, and only if you destroy all other copies of the software and the transferee agrees to the terms of the license. You may not decompile, reverse assemble, or reverse engineer the software.

Notice of Limited Warranty

The enclosed disc is warranted by Course Technology to be free of physical defects in materials and workmanship for a period of sixty (60) days from end user's purchase of the book/disc combination. During the sixty-day term of the limited warranty, Course Technology will provide a replacement disc upon the return of a defective disc.

Limited Liability

THE SOLE REMEDY FOR BREACH OF THIS LIMITED WARRANTY SHALL CONSIST ENTIRELY OF REPLACEMENT OF THE DEFECTIVE DISC. IN NO EVENT SHALL COURSE TECHNOLOGY OR THE AUTHOR BE LIABLE FOR ANY OTHER DAMAGES, INCLUDING LOSS OR CORRUPTION OF DATA, CHANGES IN THE FUNCTIONAL CHARACTERISTICS OF THE HARDWARE OR OPERATING SYSTEM, DELETERIOUS INTERACTION WITH OTHER SOFTWARE, OR ANY OTHER SPECIAL, INCIDENTAL, OR CONSEQUENTIAL DAMAGES THAT MAY ARISE, EVEN IF COURSE TECHNOLOGY AND/OR THE AUTHOR HAS PREVIOUSLY BEEN NOTIFIED THAT THE POSSIBILITY OF SUCH DAMAGES EXISTS.

Disclaimer of Warranties

COURSE TECHNOLOGY AND THE AUTHOR SPECIFICALLY DISCLAIM ANY AND ALL OTHER WARRANTIES, EITHER EXPRESS OR IMPLIED, INCLUDING WARRANTIES OF MERCHANTABILITY, SUITABILITY TO A PARTICULAR TASK OR PURPOSE, OR FREEDOM FROM ERRORS. SOME STATES DO NOT ALLOW FOR EXCLUSION OF IMPLIED WARRANTIES OR LIMITATION OF INCIDENTAL OR CONSEQUENTIAL DAMAGES, SO THESE LIMITATIONS MIGHT NOT APPLY TO YOU.

Other

This Agreement is governed by the laws of the State of Massachusetts without regard to choice of law principles. The United Convention of Contracts for the International Sale of Goods is specifically disclaimed. This Agreement constitutes the entire agreement between you and Course Technology regarding use of the software.